Praise for The CAP Equation©

"Joe Buzzello has taken every ounce of his 35 years worth of sales and sales leadership experience and distilled it down into a simple (yet incredibly powerful) formula for unlimited sales success. Violating any part of The CAP Equation, and still expecting success, is like insisting that 1+1 = 3. Conversely, if you follow the advice in this book, your chances of attaining abundance in your life go up dramatically! If you don't buy this book, and follow Joe's formula, you will have no one to blame but yourself."

- Tim Martin, Founder, SuccessIsVoluntary.com

"Joe's 3-part sales equation is simple, powerful and practical. If you build this equation, your wealth in sales will follow. Joe Buzzello has delivered a must read for anyone serious about a successful career in sales."

- Daniel P. Amos, Chairman and Chief
Executive Officer, Aflac Incorporated

"The CAP Equation© formula is Joe Buzzello's truth. If you read his book with intention, you'll receive the guidance, inspiration and knowledge you'll need to start your journey of WINNING."

- Todd Mason, Regional Sales Director
Public Sector West, Colonial Life

"Finding the right path to follow is an essential task for the budding salesperson. The CAP Equation is a systematic approach to obtaining success in sales. It serves as a solid curriculum that can take you to great heights. Joe has done a fantastic job of removing the 'noise' and has given us a system that, when followed, will ultimately lead to success!"

- Jim Sprouse, Vice President of Sales, Cain Advisory Group

"I have been around Joe for 27 years. I have always admired the way he goes about explaining this game we call sales. His book simplifies the process better than anything I've ever read on the subject. I love his simple concepts because new salespeople can apply them and see results immediately. Like the man said...it's a foolproof formula."

- Tom Giddens, Executive V.P., Director
of Sales, Aflac, U.S. Operations

"Joe has taken a complex subject, one that can often be dry, and transformed it into a richly inviting, humorous, and knowledge-filled read. His communication style is down to earth, as if a smart and funny guy is sitting right beside you having a conversation. I was both entertained and inspired to learn. Once I began turning the pages, I didn't want to put it down. Thank you, Joe, for making your formula a helpful and applicable pathway. Brilliant!"

- Deborah Carlin, *MS, PhD, NSA*
Professional Member, President & CEO
Partners In Excellence, LLC

"Joe Buzzello is one of the more accomplished sales professionals I have known in my 3+ decades in sales. He has built businesses from the ground up in one of the more difficult professions to find success in, and he has recruited, trained and coached hundreds of sales people to great success in their chosen fields. The CAP Equation is a culmination of his successes and should be required reading for all sales professionals."

- Brian T. Sullivan, Market Vice President, Humana

"Sales can be a frustrating business, but finally there's a sales formula that is simple, effective, and practical. The CAP Equation–A Foolproof Formula for Unlimited Success in Sales, reveals the secrets of Joe Buzzello who's outshined his competition for over 35 years. If your goal is to build wealth, friendships, and a brand in sales, learn from a master."

- S. Renee Smith, self-esteem and branding expert, speaker, author

"I consider Joe Buzzello a mentor as well as a friend. I am very excited that he has put his "sales brilliance" down on paper and shared it outside of his own legendary sales teams. When I was a sales manager, this would have been the ideal book for my company to give to each new sales hire, regardless of their experience. I am certain it would have decreased the time it took for them to be successful, and made my job easier."

- Hank Yuloff, President, OurMarketingGuy.com

"Joe has written a very thoughtful, intelligent, and also entertaining "user guide" for anybody interested in a sales career. But, I think this book is also just as valuable for anyone who's interested in any entrepreneurial venture. Understanding the need for focused effort, relationship development, and motivation, Joe shares his knowledge in a clear and relatable style. A great, entertaining read."

- Warren Steele, II, Senior Vice President,
US Marketing, Aflac, retired

"While Joe's CAP Equation formula is a brilliant way to break down and master the game of outside sales, this book also connects you with a truly insightful sales trainer. Joe Buzzello has been living and breathing commission-based sales for most of his life. He's passionate about helping people succeed through servant leadership, which makes him legendary. I'm stoked that he's taken the time to share his knowledge. This great resource belongs in every salesperson's library. I'm eager and excited for Joe to write a book on the subject of leadership."

- John Birsner, Owner & Managing Partner,
Ventana Fine Properties

"I have had the pleasure of working with Joe Buzzello on several different levels over the years and I'm very pleased he's finally written a book on the subject of field sales. He is a genius in his ability to clearly communicate what you HAVE to do to become successful in outside sales. If you read this book or work with Joe in any capacity, you'll be handed the purest training content from one of the best sales coaches in the country."

- Shawn Smith, Director of Field Sales Development,
Transamerica Employee Benefits

The CAP Equation

1.7.15

LOBSTER —

GO KILL IT IN 2016!

The CAP *Equation*

A Foolproof Formula for
Unlimited Success in Sales

JOE BUZZELLO

ISBN: 978-0692337578

DEDICATION

This book is dedicated to my mother, **Helen Buzzello**, who passed away on May May 8th of 2013 at the age of 92.

I recently found a note that she wrote to me. It was dated, May 4th, 1979. At the time I was eighteen years old and in the process of launching my commission sales career. The note was in her handwriting and was on the back of my business card from the auto dealership I worked at. She left it on my bedroom dresser one morning. It said:

"Enjoy every day to the fullest. Be well and happy.
You know we want life's best for you,
so keep smiling and you'll have it."

My mother was my greatest cheerleader and not a bad mentor. I did take her advice. I have tried to enjoy every day to the fullest and have kept smiling, even laughing, through these many years of work and struggles. She was supremely confident that I would have a great career in sales even when I wasn't.

I have experienced life's best and I owe a great deal of my personal and professional success to her early lessons. Her living example of how to deal with adversity with a smile on her face always amazed me. I carry the card with me, so she is always with me.

Table of Contents

PART III: ATTITUDES—C + A × P

PART IV: PIPELINE—C + A × **P**

PART V: SOLVING THE EQUATION

INTRODUCTION

The Chilidog Epiphany

"If you can't explain it simply, you don't understand it well enough."
—ALBERT EINSTEIN

The subtitle of this book makes a bold promise. It suggests that there is a formula that, if applied to your sales endeavors, will make anything less than unlimited success impossible. I'm making it sound like success in sales is as easy as 1 + 1 = 2. The plain truth of the matter is that success in your sales career *is* as certain as solving a simple math equation.

I guess that's the good news. The bad news is that many salespeople don't know what the components of the equation are, or they're unwilling to apply them to the equation. If you're lazy and don't wish to work out the equation, then this book won't help you; however, if you're willing to do some homework, I can help you become rich in sales. This book will supply you with the necessary framework of factors and also teach you how to apply them. We will even give you the answer ahead of time. Again, you simply have to be willing to do the work and commit to the formula.

I've heard the astute saying that "with every promise there should be a premise," a foundation that supports the promise. Pieces of our foundational premise lie in each chapter of this book. By chapter 3 or 4, you'll be well past any doubting Thomas mind-set that you might have had up front. You'll have moved on to the important task of learning and absorbing the parts of the equation, which is what we would prefer you focus on.

The CAP Equation© is the moniker I assigned to this cryptic sales success formula. I'd been teaching this formula for more than three decades, but I'd never given it a handle. The mathematically inspired title actually arrived in my coconut about the time I was done with the first draft of this very manuscript.

By March of 2014, I'd been interviewing, hiring, and training commission salespeople for over thirty-five years. I had built massive and legendary sales teams for several companies, but decided it was time to jump off the wheel of my current corporate VP gig and embark on a writing, speaking, and sales-coaching career. I quickly figured out that putting one's thoughts and philosophies down on paper wasn't that easy.

You see, when you've spent your entire career in the heat of battle, it's not likely you were always completely conscious of exactly *what* you did and *why* you did it, *while* you were doing it. The best and brightest in sports, entertainment, and the arts do most of their finest work unconsciously, while in "the zone." The best and brightest in sales and sales leadership can't always articulate what their secret sauce is, either.

My self-imposed hiatus from corporate America allowed me the uncommon opportunity to recall and distill the lessons I'd learned over the many years I'd been in the game. The quiet time allowed me the chance to begin to create prescriptions for success in outside sales—strategies that could be methodically duplicated and applied.

The original manuscript of this book was a solid first draft, containing much practical content, but I felt it was missing something. I sat quietly at my desk one day, waiting for inspiration. I wanted to tie things up in a bow, have a nice little hook. Then an ageless conversation popped into my brain. Please allow me to take you on a short field trip, back in time, to a long abandoned hot dog stand in Camarillo, California.

I was nineteen years old, a newly appointed sales trainer for Pennsylvania Life. The year was 1980. We sold $39 accident plans to self-employed business owners. Every new trainer was required to shadow, spend a day with, our top sales manager; hence, I was in the field with John Jamelkowski. He was intense to say the least, but could be more fully described as a finely tuned, precision sales machine. John piloted F-4 Phantoms in Vietnam, which, obviously, required a great deal of his concentration and attention. After he retired from the military, he applied all of that same focus, all of that discipline, to his chosen field—insurance sales.

He was meticulous in his preparation and approach to the work, just as if he were going through a preflight checklist for a combat mission. We didn't talk much during our field time—he didn't seem to be a real talkative guy—and honestly, I was intimidated, afraid to ask him too many questions. We marched from business to business in the local industrial parks, his eyes always sharply focused on the next door. When his work with a prospect was done—win or lose—he'd smile, walk out, and within seconds, his next target was locked into his crosshairs. John was a prodigious salesperson and even a more phenomenal sales trainer. He got more new agents into production than any of our other managers, and by almost double. He also got them into production faster than any other sales leader at our company.

We finally stopped for lunch after a grueling but profitable morning. John chose an outdoor hot dog stand so that we could eat fast and get back to work. He told me to order the chilidogs. He ordered three and had ingested all of them in the time it took me to eat just one. I knew I'd need to start asking questions quickly if I was to learn something. We'd soon be finished with our kamikaze lunch and be back cold-calling at his torrid pace. Somewhere between chomps, I worked up the nerve to ask him some questions. I choked out an inquiry about his training methods—asking him what his philosophies were and specifically how he retained far more agents than other managers. I didn't expect a long dissertation, but I also didn't anticipate his extreme brevity, either. Between big bites, John gave me a sound bite. He said to me:

"If you hire a new agent and they're failing, it'll be because of one or more of only three root causes: they're not saying the *right things*; they're not saying them in the *right way;* or they're not saying them to *enough people*. It's as simple as that, buddy boy; it's foolproof. This whole sales game is a simple mathematical equation—one I already know the answer to. You have to teach them to do two things well, and then you gotta' motivate them to multiply those two by the last one."

And that was it. He finished his third chilidog, wiped the mustard from his mouth, and we were off to his car. John had distilled his entire coaching and training model down to the three root causes of failure that he cared to monitor. Now, it took me about a month of thinking (I'm slow) to discover the inverse correlation of his statement. By pinpointing the three root causes of failure in sales, he'd also, by default, created an inverse reality—a formula of sorts for success.

If I read into what John was teaching his salespeople (and that's all I could do, given his brevity), he knew what the causes of failure were and apparently taught, inspected, and expected the *opposite* of those three prompts. He was obviously teaching them what the *right things* to say were, while also instructing them to handle themselves in the *right way*. He would then motivate them to see *enough people*. In John's way of thinking, if those three elements were marked off his preflight checklist, then the plane would get airborne, find its target, shoot it down, and get home safely. To John, there was no luck involved in sales; none was needed. Luck wasn't what a fighter pilot depended on for a successful mission.

Training salespeople wasn't some convoluted, complex, or psychological mystery to John. It was a checklist, a formula, a simple math problem, and one that he already knew the answer to. John Jamelkowski had abridged the gargantuan task of sales training to those three simple components.

It took me several more weeks to fully process my chilidog epiphany and render the lesson useful based on my personality style. I slowly adapted John's three elements into word texts and teachings that I could break down and apply. In today's sales vernacular, *"the right things"* are proficiencies or competencies, the physical part of the game: prospecting, presenting, closing, and so on. When John referred to the *"right way,"* he was commenting on the mental game, the way we think, feel, and respond under pressure. The third component, *"enough people,"* is fairly obvious. By that, John was referring to what we call our "prospecting pipeline."

The calculation I built in my head based on that conversation was that if salespeople developed all of the critical physical aspects of the game, added the necessary mind-sets, and then multiplied those by the X factor of *"enough people" in their pipeline,* they could not fail. The formula worked every time if you used it. The only people who failed were those who failed to work out the formula.

I slowly refined my no-name process, the one that John didn't even know he gave me. It became the foundational basis of my sales-training philosophy for the next thirty-five years. When a sales manager reporting to me asked for help in guiding a salesperson who was floundering, we used this simple formula to identify the root causes of the breakdown and then correct it. The sound bite John Jamelkowski delivered to me on that spring day in 1980 turned out to be just about all the insight I'd ever need to develop a foolproof formula for unlimited success in sales. It was also the formula that enabled me to become wealthy in the field of sales and sales management.

John passed on years back from a brain tumor. Our paths in the industry crossed one last time a few years before he died. We ran into each other in a lobby of a building. He was hurrying to give a presentation to a life insurance prospect. I had a chance to acknowledge him for the gift he gave me. When I tried to thank him, he simply shrugged his shoulders, not seeming to remember the casual conversation we had that day at the chilidog stand. What he did remember and commented on were the number of calls we made that day and the number of units of business he sold. He recalled those aging factoids because that's what he'd always focused on—saying the right things in the right way to enough people.

So, this ageless conversation with a man who had long since passed away entered my brain space as I sat at my writing desk. I stared at the working manuscript on the screen of my Mac when the last little part of his abbreviated lesson slapped me in the face:

"It's foolproof. This whole sales game is a simple mathematical equation—one I already know the answer to."

There it was. The "mathematical equation" line was my provocation to finally create a theme and title for the method that I'd refined and practiced for so long. I could ultimately give this formula a name and breathe life into the manuscript. I grabbed a yellow pad and began scribbling. The *right things* became Competencies; the *right way* became Attitudes; and the multiplier, *enough people* became Pipeline. I scratched out the equation:

$$C + A \times P = \textbf{Unlimited Success in Sales}$$

Eureka! With the long-lost chilidog conversation resurfacing in my brain, The CAP Equation© was born! I'd never before completely connected the three components in a logical, prearranged sequence. As I stared at my yellow pad, it struck me how vitally dependent these three areas are on each other, just like all components would be in any mathematical equation!

My flashback to the 1980 chilidog epiphany helped me distill what I'd always taught into one well-ordered formula. I knew that The CAP Equation© would greatly simplify the immense task of surviving and thriving in commission sales. I became excited about finishing the book and launching the newly minted title of my proven sales method. The theme would make it so much easier to convince new or struggling salespeople, network marketers, or entrepreneurs that all they needed to do was work on and work out a simple math equation to ensure success in selling their products or programs.

The dirty little secret is that the failure rate of new commission salespeople or network marketers is through the roof. I recently consulted with a national sales organization that reported to me that after eighteen months, only 11 percent of their new salespeople were still active. I can assure that some they reported as "active" were probably on life support, so the 11 percent figure might even be a slightly generous one.

The logical next question is: Why is the failure rate of new salespeople so high? There are a few reasons, but one of the more common is that they're given way too much to absorb up front; some of the things they're asked to spend time on are not critical to their immediate survival; and other, more critical elements are left out completely. The mass of training topics heaped onto them is usually not organized into a logical sequence, and I'm still only referring to what they're asked to learn theoretically (in the classroom or online), before they're thrust into the real world.

If they can manage to assimilate all the skill sets they're being forced to learn (critical or not), then they're typically pushed out into the field to figure out how to think, feel, and respond on their own. The new salesperson must manage a multitude of thoughts and feelings and will have to figure out how to cope with difficult emotional obstacles, such as disappointments, rejection, and the sales slumps everyone experiences.

The CAP Equation$^©$ solves this problem by presorting into three neat categories the critical elements that need to be learned and practiced. This approach can eliminate wasted motion during the first twelve to eighteen months of a salesperson's career. The CAP Equation$^©$ also places a person in a position to self-monitor and improve what matters, ensuring a jump to the next level to become a top income earner. The CAP Equation$^©$ formula is foolproof. Just as 1 + 1 will always equal 2, The CAP Equation$^©$ will always equal unlimited success if you are faithful to its integrity.

I was recently in the company of the gifted speaker, trainer, and best-selling author Jack Canfield. You might recognize Jack as the co-creator of the *Chicken Soup for the Soul* book series. Jack is also the author of *The Success Principles: How to Get from Where You Are to Where You Want to Be.* Jack had briefly reviewed The CAP Equation$^©$ materials and methodology and commented to me that he loves formulas because they simplify things that people have a tendency to make complex. Jack then told me that one of his favorite sayings is, "The principles always work if you always work the principles."

Jack's right, and the best news is that The CAP Equation$^©$ method of governing your sales career is certainly a principled approach. There is no hocus pocus involved, but there is some work to do in the development of proficiencies and the adoption of new thought processes. Are you ready to get started?

PART I

Foundational Concepts

CHAPTER 1

Pump in the Desert

Resolving to Make It

> *"Patience and perseverance have a magical effect before which difficulties disappear and obstacles vanish."*
>
> — **JOHN QUINCY ADAMS**

Before we dive into the breakdown and study of *C,* Competencies, *A* Attitudes, and *P* Pipeline, I will offer up a few chapters of preparatory thought, some foundational principles that will set your success in motion. I would like you to be in the right mental place to receive the information in this book, and Part I will offer you the very important groundwork for that objective. In this chapter, I will challenge you to adopt a resolute mind-set toward the career you've chosen, and I will demonstrate why that one mind-set is so critical.

3

To digress, I never set out on an intentional path to make millions in commission sales. It would be cool if I could spin a story about how I laid out a careful career plan, did market research, and then chose the perfect company to work for. I could lie to you, tell you I had the best of mentorship and hit the ground running, my trajectory to the top assured. It would be awesome to share that kind of story with you—but I can't. The fact of the matter is, I stumbled into the world of commission sales, received some decent training, but still had to figure out a lot of things on my own. My first year was painful, and most of the salespeople who started when I did left within the first year with their tails stuck firmly between their legs. I believe I was simply too dumb to quit, or maybe I should simply thank God for my stubborn nature.

What if you simply decided that you were going to make it, stick, and stay? What if you made up your mind that you were going to put on the blinders and persevere in commission sales, become skilled at your craft, regardless of the pain? How would that change things? This first lesson is about how being stubborn isn't necessarily a bad thing if you have chosen a career in commission sales.

For the purpose of this book, when I use the term *commission sales*, it denotes an outside sales position, one without base compensation or a W2 sales position with little or no salary. It won't matter what product or service you're selling or what distribution model you're working under. These concepts will work with direct-to-consumer sales, business-to-business sales (B2B), and also multilevel marketing. (MLM). The principles discussed in this book are interchangeable and universal. I wrote this book with four types of men and women in mind:

1. Those considering a commission sales or MLM career
2. People already in sales but relatively new to the game
3. Sales veterans who might be stalled at a certain level
4. All leaders and trainers of salespeople

The organization you join—as well meaning as they might be—won't be able to change the inescapable odds stacked against you, and most don't even try. (More on that subject in the next chapter) There will be a period of time when you starve until your commissions start flowing, and some of the work you'll have to do to be successful will feel excruciatingly unnatural.

There is an upside, however. The rewards can be life altering. You can become financially free—a millionaire and beyond if you care to—creating a lifestyle you've only dreamed of. You can transform yourself into a respected professional, the self-confident person who you always knew you could be.

I know that you've taken notice of the lifestyles that are available to successful salespeople. It might be the insurance agent with the great tan who drives a new BMW. It could be the pharmaceutical rep who takes Fridays off to play golf. We've seen the well-dressed realtor cruising around in her new Mercedes, top down, sun in her face; she's taking a tennis and spa day in the middle of the week. These prosperous professionals don't have to punch a clock; they make their own hours, working as much as they want or as little as they wish.

It all looks very enticing; however, we're typically only seeing the finished product. We're seeing the end result of a great amount of dedication, hard work, and disciplined thought. We have no idea what they sacrificed up front.

This finished product is appealing to us and it's easy to fixate on. It can be intoxicating if we fail to consider what these professionals invested of themselves to get to where they are. You can rest assured that the superstar salesperson suffered a steep learning curve. Most of their pain, hard lessons, failures, and rejections probably came during the first twelve to twenty-four months of their careers. The price they paid to become a success in commission sales was front-loaded. One of my favorite sayings is, "If the first year doesn't kill you, then you'll be fine."

The sobering truth is that the majority of people entering commission sales will crash and burn (quit) before the one-year mark. Consider this grave paradox for a moment. I've told you that most of the pertinent lessons to be learned occur during year one. However, I've also told you that most wide-eyed, hopeful salespeople don't last that long.

As a way to better understand this enigma, let me use this analogy. An eager salesperson wanders the barren desert looking for water, and he comes upon a pump. The pump represents his sales vehicle and its rewards. He wants to taste the refreshing water and starts pumping the handle. After a while, a trickle comes out. It's enough to keep his lips wet but not enough to quench his thirst. He stays at it, working the pump handle tentatively. Eventually though, when he's unsure of when the water will gush out and what specific effort it will take, his despairing nature takes hold, and he walks away.

The truth is, he did most of the hard work already—paid most of the price—just before quitting. The water was rising to the top, and the pump would've soon delivered the payload, but he didn't hang in there long enough to reap the reward. He walked away thirsty and defeated because he wasn't sure when the water was going to flow out on a regular basis. He had no clue what specific skill sets were required and what level of effort it was going to take to make that result happen.

It's not all his fault; the buzzards flying overhead were making crazy, distracting noises. He might have been running low on cash reserves, might even have had well-meaning loved ones chirping in his ear to "get out of that crazy business" or to "get a real job." There wasn't anybody he trusted enough to give him the straight facts. There was nobody standing nearby, telling him exactly what to do, how to think, and how many more times he'd need to work the pump handle before the steady flow gushed out.

If only there could have been a mystic figure standing next to him, whispering, "You're doing the right things; the water's coming...you're 50 percent there...you're 75 percent there." If this cosmic mentor were there to walk him through the process—demystify it—the outcome would've been different. That new salesperson would have hung in there, knowing he was on target to win the game. The good news is that the proven concepts contained in The CAP Equation© (and a few carefully selected coaches) will be those demystifying elements for you.

If you survive year one in commission sales, your chances of sustained, long-term success increase exponentially. Through The CAP Equation©

sales methodology, we will expose all the landmines and teach you how to step around them. This book will dispel the myths that exist and also challenge you to think and act differently than most neophytes do. We promise to proffer no *untested* theories.

According to *Webster's Dictionary*, a theory is: "An idea that is suggested or presented as possibly true, but that is not known or proven to be true." Our theories have been tested and are known to be true.

I've spent my entire professional life in commission sales and sales leadership. I've interviewed over seven thousand potential sales candidates and had the pleasure to personally mentor and coach over two thousand of them. I'm fairly certain I know why some make it in outside sales and why a lot more people don't. Like a popular TV commercial states, "It's not that complicated."

Through application of the formula in this book, you will learn the practices and mind-sets that will get you through year one, or help you restart your sales career. We will get that water gushing out of that pump in the desert for you. You won't have to struggle for years, pumping the pump, until you figure it out on your own. The CAP Equation© takes the guesswork out of the game and can set you on a path of success that is predictable.

So, let's go back to that series of questions I asked a few pages back and tweak them a little. What if you simply resolved to stay at the pump until the water gushed out, knowing that it would? What if you decided up front that you were going to persevere and learn your craft, regardless of the pain, because the pain was temporary and minimal in relation to the vast rewards?

How would this mind-set change things for you? Here's hoping that you are purposefully stubborn, because if you are not, you might wander away from the pump defeated when you could have just as easily drank from it.

CHAPTER 2

Survival Mode

They Don't Teach It in School

"Learning is not compulsory... neither is survival."

— **W. Edwards Deming,**

author, management consultant

While chapter 1 was about being stubborn, keeping your head down and blinders on, this chapter challenges you to open your eyes to your surroundings so that you are prepared to survive them. We also talk about three characteristics that will be most instrumental to your survival in the sales jungle.

I know you've heard the saying, "It's a jungle out there." Well, if you're new in commission sales, it will seem like a jungle. Danger will be lurking everywhere, savage beasts will be ready to ambush you, and you'll quickly run low on food and water. You'll have to learn how to survive, and the conditions you'll be asked to exist in will be very difficult.

I believe that today's work environment is very much a mirror of the times: uncertain and unstable. As you traverse this fast-paced landscape, you will naturally begin to develop attitudes based on your environment, and those outlooks will surely play out in your behavior.

It's important that you understand how things have evolved in the workplace, especially in sales. In the past, I was involved with sales teams that were focused on the planning and execution of long-term growth objectives. I was associated with organizations that were generally places where careers were born and legacies were created. I've had the opportunity to work with a few great Fortune 500˚ companies, such as Aflac, where teamwork, unity, and collaboration were encouraged and advancement possibilities were real.

In today's world, long-term business goals are sometimes eclipsed by short-term personal goals. As a result, you will have to adapt to a habitat where everything is a priority and time management is unmanageable. This will require you to focus on surviving the unknown long enough to stay in the game and win.

As you observe the behaviors in your culture, you'll take note that others might also be in *survival mode*. In the past, it was easier to strike a friendship with people at your level. In today's tension-filled environment, people might only spend time with those who can help their careers. As a result, meaningful relationships are much harder to forge.

The survival-mode atmosphere has also made it increasingly difficult to collaborate because each person has urgent issues to cope with. When people do meet, they tend to posture and sell themselves rather than advance the organizational goals. This kind of self-promotion is the ultimate sign of survival-mode thinking, and it creates a fierce, dog-eat-dog mentality.

The reason I'm harping on these potential undercurrents is that I want you to be cognizant of what might be going on around you. You can easily become a victim of someone else's survival strategy and begin to lose faith in your company, or worse, take your eye off the prize. They don't teach survival mode in school, and most of us don't begin our sales careers hoping to isolate and work solely for our own short-term goals, but as survival mode takes hold in more organizations, it will be important for you to recognize it and know what the rules are.

Let's move on to those key survival characteristics we referenced. It would be easy to draft a long list of specific attributes, philosophies, and attitudes, ones key to your survival. Some companies depend on complicated aptitude tests as a main part of their hiring practices, believing these tests are predictive of who will succeed. I believe these tests can be somewhat reliable indicators of future success; however, I did fail one of these tests once when interviewing with a major insurance carrier. The humor in this is that I failed the test at a time when I'd already become a successful sales professional and trainer.

Taking into consideration that complex profiling tests are sometimes faulty, but allowing that you'd like to know what it really takes to survive in sales, please allow me to offer you this short list of attributes. I've boiled it down to three major qualities that will make all the difference for you.

LONG-TERM THINKING—THE RAMP-UP PERIOD

Regardless of what they told you during your interview process, there's always a *ramp-up* period in commission-based sales. Your income might suffer while you're learning your trade. This isn't a bad thing; consider the ramp-up period an extension of your education—an advanced investment in yourself. If you're looking for immediate gratification or to get-rich-quick in commission sales, you might not last.

You can, however, get rich slowly. The investment you make in yourself will be well worth it if you are focusing on all of the right things, and we intend to make sure you are focused on the right things through your understanding of The CAP Equation©.

COACHABILITY

You're probably venturing into an industry or joining a company that you know little about. Even if you have some experience, you'll probably still have to accept that you need help from others. It would be prudent to park your ego at the training-room door and become coachable and trainable. If you aren't easily coachable, then you'll most likely have to change your outlook. Sometimes, becoming coachable means you must first become humble, which you can't learn in a book. That will simply be a decision you have to make.

In my experience, with regard to coaching salespeople, most only realize the payback of change *after* the change has occurred. If we are lucky enough to find true mentors, we sometimes resist them until we see tangible results. The *Catch 22* here is that we only get results if we don't resist our coaches. Surrendering control takes faith. Your life must be lived *forward*, but can only be fully understood and appreciated when you're able to look *backward*; hence, faith is also an element in becoming coachable.

TOUGH-MINDEDNESS

We are all emotional creatures to some degree, but if you are the sort of person who becomes depressed when things don't go well or when your ideas are rejected, you'll have a difficult time surviving in sales. The best and brightest salespeople operate in a level mode with unwavering attitudes. They never get too *up,* and they never get too *down.* They can almost seem robotic, but all they've done is develop logical coping mechanisms for themselves. Later in this book, we will teach you how to adopt a different perspective of the triggers that can create disruptive emotions. You will learn how to respond to impediments and difficulties analytically versus emotionally. We will convey a set of truths on this subject so powerful, that when practiced, your entire sales career can transform.

In this chapter, we have made you aware of the cultural landmines that might exist, and we've challenged you to become a long-term thinker, coachable, and tough-minded. These are critical traits to your survival; in fact, I've rarely seen a person fail in commission sales if these traits were acquired and practiced.

Let's move on to the next chapter. Let's talk about the odds—which end of the odds you want to be on, and how to tip those odds in your favor.

CHAPTER 3

Odds and Ends

Getting to the Other Side

"When something is important enough, you'll do it even if the odds of success are not in your favor."

—**ELON MUSK,** inventor, co-founder, PayPal, Tesla Motors

I am a pessimist by nature. It's in my DNA. I believe I inherited the gift of suspicion from my mother, Helen. She was a child of the Great Depression. She grew up poor, waiting in soup and bread lines. When I was a kid, I watched my mother clip coupons and look for items on sale. She'd make my dad stop at the day-old bread store on the way home from church each Sunday. She'd stock up because the loaves there were five cents cheaper than at our regular market. She acted as if she didn't know where our next meal was coming from. While we weren't rich, we did eat well and live comfortably, but she still had a mild form of paranoia.

I believe she lived in a constant mind-set that the odds were against her. My theory is that she stayed in this mind-set in order to stay on her game. Being paranoid and pinching every penny was her edge. She'd gone to sleep on an empty stomach more than once as a child of poor immigrant parents. Her family did survive, all of the siblings eventually finding good professions after the war. They beat the odds by working two, even three jobs at a time. They refused to act poor or remain poor. They knew the odds were against them, but they also knew they had to outwork and outthink everyone else around them to get to the other end of those odds. The scripting from her childhood apparently never left my mom. She was determined never to be on the wrong end of the odds again.

My point in telling you about my mom's attitude is that I believe it would be prudent for you to acknowledge that the odds are inherently against you becoming wealthy in commission sales. If I can first convince you of that, you'll naturally begin to look for ways to bend the odds in your favor. You'll try to find an *edge* here or there. Hopefully, you'll also look at the smaller percentage of people making big money in commission sales and ask the question, how are they *thinking* and *acting* differently than those who fail? If I can get you asking these kinds of questions, you will naturally want to *model* the actions and thought processes of top producers.

This isn't a long chapter, but don't judge its importance based on its length. I won't go into detail on how we'll help you beat the odds in this chapter, but I will tell you what the odds *are* and present a foundational concept, one that we will refer to repeatedly throughout this book. This concept will also come in handy for you as you progress beyond the initial stages of your sales career.

Allow me to introduce an Italian man who developed a few interesting theories. Vilfredo Pareto was an engineer by trade but is better known as an economist and philosopher. His most notable contribution to economics was in the study of income distribution. He popularized the term *elite* in the context of social analysis. Because I am about to tell you that not all commission income is distributed equally within your organization and that there will be elite salespeople, Vilfredo and his principles are a worthwhile study.

Pareto initially developed his principle by observing that 20 percent of the pea pods in his garden yielded 80 percent of the peas. He then learned that 80 percent of the land in Italy was owned by only 20 percent of the population. Years later, the term *Pareto Principle* was coined and studied by many economists and philosophers, including Joseph Juran. You may simply recognize this principle as the *80-20 rule.*

Other names for this law are the *law of the vital few* and the *principle of factor sparsity.* We'll just call it the 80-20 rule for our needs. Basically, the 80-20 rule is a cause-and-effect law that states:

Roughly 80 percent of all effects come from 20 percent of the causes.

As previously stated, we'll reference this law several times in this book when explaining and teaching The CAP Equation©; however, let's broaden the application as it pertains to business, sales, and entrepreneurs so that you can get a better handle on the concept. How about this application: 80 percent of a company's profits sometimes come from only 20 percent of its customers. Consider also that 80 percent of a company's complaints might come from only 20 percent of its customers. More on topic, 80 percent of a company's sales come from only 20 percent of its products. And most importantly, for our needs, consider that 80 percent of an industry's sales are made by only 20 percent of its salespeople.

This principle would support my theory that the odds are stacked against you from the start. If 80 percent of all commissions were going to flow to only 20 percent of the elite salespeople, why would you even start down this road? Probably because you are deluded enough to believe that you can crack the 20 percent's code and become one of them. Here's the good news: there is a code, and it's not unreasonable to think you can crack it.

We will supply you with all the necessary tools to move over to the margin of the 20 percent if that's what you choose to do. What I want to make sure you understand at this juncture is that, in sales, there are *haves* and *have-nots*. The commission sales game does not operate in a socialist environment. In fact, most of the time, it doesn't even seem like a fair situation for a new person. I've seen the massive chasm between the elite and the rest of the bunch several times in my sales career. In our business, the 80-20 rule seems to rear its ugly head 100 percent of the time.

For example, at my very first sales job at a Ford dealership, it became immediately obvious that there were a dozen salespeople who were killing it—making a relative fortune—and the rest of us were left to pick up scraps. It wasn't any different when I began selling accident insurance policies in 1979 for Penn Life. There were a few elite salespeople who were number one, two or three on the big production board every week. The rest of us simply settled for numbers four through twenty on the *other* production board in the hallway. I did elbow my way onto the big board a few times. That was sweet; but it didn't happen as consistently as I wanted. I hadn't completely figured things out yet, but I was close to cracking the code!

When I did get my name posted on the big board at Penn Life, they asked me to stand up and talk about my week. I was thrilled to be able to taste this morsel of success and motivate others. It felt awesome being recognized as an elite performer on those occasions. I was beginning to feel like I could jump to the other side.

The most dramatic example of the 80-20 rule I've ever seen was when I was involved in a multilevel marketing business in the early 1980s. I began this venture as a part-time distributor during the summer of 1982, and immediately perceived a stark class difference existed. There were definitely haves and have-nots. The separation was as big as the Grand Canyon. On one rim of the canyon sat hopeful, energetic distributors dutifully attending meetings, selling products, and trying to recruit others. Most of the hard-working distributors were couples, working full-time jobs and then putting another twenty hours a week into their home-based businesses on top of that. They were plodding along, but in most cases, their expenses were more than their commissions.

On the other side of the canyon sat the fat cats. These elite distributors were living the top 1 percent lifestyle in the United States. They drove luxury vehicles, sometimes decorating their driveways with three or four of them at a time. They were living in palatial mansions. They were financially free. Most had quit their real jobs and were traveling the world, staying in five-star hotels. The top distributors in that multilevel marketing business didn't seem to be more intelligent than the 80 percent; they'd just cracked the code; they were, in essence, practicing The CAP Equation©.

By the summer of 1982, I'd been in commission sales for three years and had the game mostly figured out. I had a little more than a clue of how to get to the "promised land." I'd even developed some very solid skills in the training and leadership area. I had begun to read books like my life depended on it. I'd read most of the classic books on sales and sales management, many of them two and three times over.

It was during the summer of 1982 that I took a deeper look at the haves and have-nots around me. I was somewhere around the bubble. It was then that my self-confidence and self-esteem levels rose to a place that signaled to me I was ready. I was no longer content being mediocre, just making a living. I wanted to develop wealth; I wanted to become one of them. I decided to jump the fence—go to the other side—and become part of Pareto's 20 percent permanently.

You recall that I mentioned the fighter pilot, John Jamelkowski, in the introduction of this book. I had swallowed his chilidog-fueled lesson and made it my own. I'd slowly refined the three main components so that I was able to make a good living in sales and also teach others how to do so. But there was one last thing holding me back. It was a faulty attitude. I had to sharpen my distant vision. I had to simply see myself as one of the 20 percent. I had to convince myself I belonged there.

By the summer of 1982, I was ready to commit to that. I was ready to cast off any actions or thoughts that were unproductive, any practices that were prohibiting me from making the final leap. I had earlier reasoned that modeling only some of the pieces of The CAP Equation© would not allow the formula to work. I want to stress again that if you omit any of the components, the equation fails.

At that point in my career, my thoughts had started to become well organized. I was ready to transform them into a substantial monetary reality. It took me a total of three years of pain and struggle to figure it all out, but I finally did.

There was one other thing that occurred during the summer of 1982. I'd added a mentor to my stable, one who challenged me and pushed me way out of my comfort zone. He was not only part of the 20 percent; he was the top 1 percent of the 20 percent. He allowed me inside, exposing all of the nuances that the 20 percent master. He handed me the last few keys to unlock their code, the greatest being the value that they placed on their time.

Before we begin to break down the core Competencies needed, allow me one more preparatory and foundational chapter. Let's take a look at how the top 20 percent value and manage their precious time.

CHAPTER 4

The Majors

Your Valuable Time

"Time is the school in which we learn, time is the fire in which we burn."
— **DELMORE SCHWARTZ,** American poet

Time is a funny thing. Some people think we can actually *manage it*. I still, to this day, use the term "time management." But we don't and can't *manage* time at all. We are best served to think about this differently.

We can only *manage ourselves* inside of small chunks of time.

I promise you we're going to build and solve The CAP Equation©, but first we need to explore this one final foundational topic. It is one that doesn't fit neatly into any single component, but overlays all of them. This subject can be considered both a Competency and an Attitude. It will also influence how well you manage your Pipeline. It is such a foundational subject that without a disciplined approach in this area, you could be functioning at an expert level in all of the other practices we teach and still crash and burn. Of course, you know we are talking about your valuable time.

I'd like to share a real-life lesson, one that I learned one morning over pancakes. I was the last person at the breakfast meeting—the back booth at Denny's. I had made the mistake of leaving my calendar open too long. The man that was mentoring me saw it.

"Holy *crap*," my coach yelled.

He was hovering over me, glaring down at my 8 x 10 week-at-a-glance spiral-bound calendar. (If you were alive back in the '80s, you might recall the behemoth paper calendars that we lugged around with us. There were no mobile devices, no cloud, no electronic or digital anything. Our calendars were pulp and ink.) He scrutinized my empty calendar as he continued his invective.

"I could go *snow-blind* from all the white space in your calendar. Where are your appointments for the week? Please tell me you just didn't put them in your calendar yet."

I didn't have a great answer for him. I'd taken a long weekend—a weekend that started the previous Wednesday.

"Hey, don't worry," I promised. "I got this handled. My week will come together."

I was dancing and he knew it. Even if I hit the phone and spent all day dialing for dollars, he knew I wasn't going to be able to fill my empty calendar. He knew my week was already doomed to be a shaky one. He ushered me outside, clearly not happy with me. He'd spent a lot of time mentoring me, and I knew he didn't like wasting time, mostly his. He rubbed his forehead with both hands, like I was his biggest headache. I knew he was preparing to rip into me.

"Listen Joe, you're a talented kid—a diamond in the rough. You can be great. But talent alone won't cut it. You have to value your time and manage yourself better along with your calendar. You can't skate or slack off, and I won't let you."

And then he said the twelve words that I've repeated a million times when trying to convince new salespeople to take their business seriously:

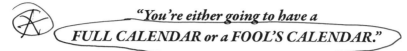

"You're either going to have a
FULL CALENDAR or a FOOL'S CALENDAR."

I got his message loud and clear. I knew that as my calendar went, so did my income. There is no way to cheat the numbers, shortcut the system, or produce consistent results without a full and well-organized calendar. Success simply doesn't happen without a firm grasp of time and calendar-management concepts.

In this chapter, we look at a few of the fundamental philosophies you must adopt to manage yourself and your calendar to its maximum efficiency. I'm not going to make this subject complex. I've read books on time and calendar management that I couldn't even follow. I'm simply going to give you a handful of proven principles that absolutely work. I'm going to go deep on a few points that are critical to your early success in sales—the factors that will help you stick and stay. Let's get started with a short list of absolutes on this topic.

DON'T HIDE BEHIND YOUR E-CALENDAR

I know we all have electronic calendars in these most tech-infested of times, and they're great. Being able to put an appointment into our mobile device and have it sync to our tablet, laptop, or desktop via the cloud reeks of awesomeness. There is a major downside, however. As I've coached salespeople over recent years, I've noticed it's become tougher to analyze their return on time invested. It is almost impossible for a coach to know what's really going on without being able to do a visual inspection of a person's calendar. It's too easy for people to give lip service but never share their actual calendar with their coaches. The only reason my mentor was able to help me that day at Denny's was that he was able to see my calendar. My lack of calendar mastery was transparent.

My first advice to you on this subject is that you *schedule time with the person coaching you, then print out or send your coach access to your weekly and monthly work-related calendar.* Show your coach where you are spending your time. Allow your mentor to coach you in regard to those calendar activities. If all other cylinders are firing (you know your product, pitch, have solid attitudes, etc.), but you're squandering precious time with an empty appointment calendar, then you're defeating your purpose.

MAJOR IN THE MAJORS

That same mentor—the guy who screamed at me in Denny's—also championed one other idiom that I have since used faithfully. He was driving us to a meeting one day and he questioned how, and what, I was doing with my time. He caught me in a web of conversation that revealed to him that I was busy performing low-priority tasks. He paused for a moment and then said, "People fail in commission sales, sometimes fail even though they have decent skills. Ya know why?" I shook my head obediently, and he replied:

"Because they major in the minors. That's why."

He was telling me that many new salespeople spend a *major* amount of time on things of *minor* importance. They have their priorities all mixed up, intentional or not. They don't have the wisdom to determine what items need to be given weight in their calendar and which activities do not merit weight.

The first thing you'll want to do as a new salesperson is *determine what activities should have priority in your calendar.* Based on what you're selling and how you are selling it, this can vary. While I suggest you seek counsel from your hierarchy or manager, I can also tell you that your top three priorities shouldn't deviate much from the classic top 3:

1. **Prospecting**—filling your calendar with appointments
2. **Presenting and Following Up**—with qualified prospects
3. **Closing a Sale**—writing the order

What's priority #4 you ask? There isn't one. I've certainly seen new salespeople come up with items and activities to fill their calendars. I've witnessed new salespeople doing anything but the top 3. It was almost as if they were trying to *avoid* becoming successful by focusing on all of the wrong things! If you're going to thrive, you must *major* in the *majors*.

The noted author, Dr. Stephen R. Covey, has written many useful books. He is certainly on my recommended reading list. I was greatly impacted by one of his analogies, *The Big Rocks of Life*. In the way of a story, he tells about an expert who was speaking to a group of business students. To drive home a point, the speaker used an illustration of placing "rocks" in a gallon mason jar. That jar represents our time. The speaker placed the rocks (priorities) in the jar, all the way up to the top, and then asked the group if the jar were full.

It was a trick question. He then produced some gravel (representing lesser priorities) and poured those smaller stones into the mason jar. They filled the voids. He repeated the question, asked again if the jar were full; some in the class had caught onto him. He then proceeded to dump sand and also water into the jar, allowing the other, smaller substances to sink into the receptacle and fill the empty space.

One student thought that the point was that no matter how full your day was, you could always do more. The presenter shot him down and advised that this wasn't the point of the example at all. The point the speaker was trying to make was that if you don't put the big rocks in first, you'll never get them in at all because your jar will be filled with all of the other, less important stuff.

Whether we refer to your urgent business activities as "*big rocks*," "*priorities*," or "*majors*," it all amounts to the same thing: *Most new salespeople have difficulty identifying these critical items and getting them done early in their daily and weekly work cycles.* The "majors" tend to be the most uncomfortable tasks—like cold-calling; hence, they are the things that newbies unconsciously try to avoid. Your natural instincts might lead you to practice the tasks that are easy or comfortable. Fight that instinct. Start each day tracking the things that are most challenging for you, get them done, then, as the day rolls on, fill in with less impactful and easier items.

PRIME TIME VERSUS NON-PRIME TIME

As important as identifying what *major* and *minor* activities look like, there is one other calendar skill you must master: You must identify your *prime time* and guard it with your life. Prime time starts for most B2B salespeople around 8:00–8:30 a.m. and ends around 5:00–5:30 p.m. This is the time they can find a decision maker in their offices. Prime time can extend into the evening if you also sell to individuals in their homes. It varies based on what you sell and whom you sell it to, but it is fairly easy to define.

Pros know what prime time is. They don't do anything of minor importance during this time. They relegate those items to *non-prime time* only. I can also tell you about the salespeople who came in late each day, drank coffee, loitered, and took long lunches. They had no concept of prime time and little or no desire of guarding it or using it well. Worse, they were perfectly happy to drag unsuspecting newbies into their black hole of sales death.

I've read many books on calendar and time management and spent endless hours discussing the subject with highly successful people. I can assure you that pros don't let anything or anyone distract them from using their prime time for the three major priorities. If this is the only thing you know about time management, you are light years ahead of the 80 percent.

SUNDAY NIGHT LIVE (Weekly Calendar Fine-Tuning)

What do you do Sunday night? I can tell you what top performers in sales do. They work on their calendar for the upcoming week. Early on in my sales career, I was coached to spend half an hour each Sunday night analyzing my week. It was my *pregame*. I would determine how effective my game plan was, identifying holes and planning how I'd fill them. Then, with a plan in mind, I could always spend some time on Monday morning fine-tuning it. The four-step process I always employed when building and reviewing my calendar looked like this:

①. Print out or view my weekly calendar
②. *Identify* my available *prime* selling hours
③. Mark or *block out* those hours
④. Schedule only *major* priorities during that time

Wednesday was *halftime*. The objective in doing a midweek checkup was that I never wanted to lose an entire week to calendar neglect or poorly placed priorities. I always asked myself the following questions:

- How is my week shaping up?
- Am I on target to meet my stated objectives?
- If not, why not, and in what area?
- How quickly can I get back on target?

Friday was *postgame*. I'd reflect on everything accomplished and not accomplished. I would determine what corrections I'd need to make for the following week. I'd begin to look ahead to the upcoming week. Managing the effectiveness of your calendar is a fluid practice. True professionals monitor their calendars 24/7.

COFFEE ISN'T EVEN FOR CLOSERS ANYMORE
(Time-Wasting Office Traps)

I'm going to reference the sad bunch of characters in that classic movie, *Glengarry Glen Ross*. In that one infamous scene, Shelly, the old, washed-up salesperson, casually gets up from his desk, waltzes over to the coffeemaker, and pours a big, steamy cup while being admonished by the Alec Baldwin character. "Coffee is for closers; *put the cup down!*" the character yells. Alec Baldwin's character was imploring the lazy crew to stop socializing, complaining—or whatever they were doing in the office—and get to work.

If you find yourself in the office during *prime-time* selling hours and without a qualified prospect, you might be squandering your time. There are many subtle time wasters around the office. It's a comfortable and warm environment, and the field is not. But the time-sucking land mines are everywhere in the office. Stay out of the office and get your butt in the field!

I think you understand the importance of these paradigms and techniques, but I'm not quite done with the subject of time just yet. I want to address another facet of time. This aspect will be closer to home.

It's not uncommon in our world to applaud workaholics. Hold them up as heroes. You've seen these types of highly charged entrepreneurs or independent salespeople. They race around, cantankerously announcing that they are exhausted, "so busy," "swamped," "slammed." They'll tell you there isn't enough time to get everything done. They think they're successful, you think they're successful, and they definitely seem prosperous to the world; however, if you think about it, that really doesn't make much sense. Can you truly be successful if you can't slow down for a moment and reap the benefits of your hard work?

Look, I'm probably the last one who should point fingers. I ran sixty-plus hours a week for close to two decades, never taking a true vacation. (A cell phone or beeper was always strapped to my side.) When I began to take stock of my life, I realized that I had not taken a vacation longer than seven days since I'd begun my commission-selling career in 1979. I'm not sure I was completely present to my wife and daughter during my go-go years. I still struggle with that now, even in a semiretirement mode.

As I have slowed a bit and crossed the line, joining the fifty-plus club, I've begun to look at things a little differently. I've begun to value my time contrarily, placing more emphasis on the things that are really important to me. I'm not suggesting you lessen your commitment to your career or organization. I'm simply suggesting that it might be possible for you to strike more balance in your life. Here are some thoughts on the real value of your time.

MORE CLARITY—BETTER JUDGMENT

Independent business owners and salespeople say that the reason they became independent is to have control of their time. The stark reality is that when you begin your sales career or venture, you're going to have to pump the pump harder than you ever dreamed of. The more you build, do or sell, the more decisions you have to make. Come Saturday, it's not uncommon for these committed business owners to wake up and immediately go to their work caves.

My experience tells me that when I slow down on the weekend and do something fun, I'm able to develop more clarity about business issues. I find that when I take the time to reboot, I am able to make better decisions and find the solutions I need on Monday morning.

Round Yourself Out

Most hard-charging salespeople or entrepreneurs understand that passion is a vital element to becoming successful. It's also important to follow your passions outside of work. Use your weekends to explore your creative side. The activity doesn't really matter; what's important is to take a break. This non-work-related pursuit will make you happier and a better-rounded person.

You—Unplugged

It's hard to clear your head or relax if you are tethered to your personal electronic devices 24/7. Technology has made it difficult for us to unplug. One small step you can take is keeping your devices out of your hands and in a drawer at least on the weekends for longer blocks of time.

When I recently spent time with the best-selling author Jack Canfield, he mentioned that during a "free day" (that's a day he does *no* work) he doesn't have any electronic devices near him. He's truly unplugged! After he sized me up, Jack joked that he didn't think I was the type who could easily set down my phone and take a real free day. I'm trying to prove him wrong...getting closer by the day.

If you think about it, most of us in sales aren't saving lives. A patient isn't going to die if we miss a call, text, or e-mail. Every request, lead, or service call will still be there when we get back to our desks. We live in a competitive world. Taking a break—some unaffected free time—will allow us to take a hard look at where we are and determine where we want to go next.

FUNCTIONAL FAMILY

If you gain wealth, recognition, stature, and power, and then you lose your family, what have you really gained? You work hard because you want to give yourself and your family the best of everything. Use the weekends to spend time with them. Take time out to get together with friends and socialize. Success means nothing if you're not able to share it with the people you love.

THE HOURGLASS

I have a small hourglass on my bookcase in my home office. Once in a while, I'll turn it upside down and watch as the sands drop through the small hole. At first, the sand seems to move slowly, but near the end, it seems to move faster. Then the hourglass becomes still. There is no more sand, no more time.

The small hourglass is my reminder that God has given all of us a limited amount of time. Time well spent with loved ones or doing the things that put a smile on our faces is by far the most valuable commodity we have. You don't hear people on their deathbeds say; "I wish I could go into my office just one more Saturday and clean up some files." What they wish they could do is have one more day—heck, maybe just one more hour—with the people they love.

If you are still not convinced that time well spent is more valuable than money, please read this poem written by Rinku Tiwari:

To realize the value of a year,
Ask a student who failed in the exam.
To realize the value of a month,
Ask a mother how she spends the first month with her child.

To realize the value of a week,
Ask a patient how he recovers from his illness.
To realize the value of an hour,
Ask a student who missed the class.
To realize the value of a minute,
Ask a person who missed the train.
To realize the value of a second,
Ask a person who saved you from an accident.
To realize the value of a millisecond,
Ask a person who has won the medal in the competition.
Spend your time well.

Okay, do you have these first few chapters wired? Good...then it's time to start building and solving The CAP Equation©.

PART II

Competencies - C + A × P

CHAPTER 5

The Right Things

Why Mastering Competencies is Critical

"The quality of a person's life is in direct proportion to their commitment to excellence, regardless of their chosen field of endeavor."

— **VINCE LOMBARDI,** legendary NFL coach

One of the chronic spectacles I've witnessed during my tenure in sales is the miserable failure of people who seemed so smart and who interviewed so well. They seemed so capable during the hiring and training process. These are people you fall in love with. They seem to have solid enthusiasm and are willing to go out and work, and then...*wham*! They fall flat on their faces! Sometimes, they exit loudly; sometimes, they slink away quietly; but they're gone, and they seemed to have so much promise on the surface.

I'll use an example to illustrate this. I'll refer to the person as Rick Palmer (not his real name). I hired Palmer early in my leadership tenure, at a time when I could still be fooled by what I saw on the surface. Palmer was an extremely personable guy in his mid twenties. He had some sales experience and was quite articulate. He blew us away during the interview process. I labeled him a *"can't miss"* prospect, a sure thing to be my next superstar. I couldn't wait to get him out in the field and to begin working with him.

After he completed his license requirements, he enrolled in our new-agent sales class, supposedly doing the work required to learn our products and services. He was also required to learn our basic approach and presentation, and the rebuttals to all of the basic objections.

He completed his classroom training, and we made it out into the field to start calling on prospects. I made the first three walk-ins to small business owners and had the good fortune to get a "yes" on the third attempt. I instructed him that he would make the next few approaches, and then we'd stop to have a lunch and talk about our morning's results.

That's when it happened. He froze up. He locked his feet to the ground like a dog not wanting to get into the bathtub. He didn't want to expose the fact that he hadn't done his homework. He made some excuse about being out late, not getting enough sleep the previous night. He asked that I make a few more walk-ins so he could watch me. When I tried to role-play with him over lunch, he froze up again and tried to change the topic. He wasn't able to role-play with me because he hadn't memorized or internalized any of the required front talk or the basic presentation text of our products.

He'd made a lot of friends during his training at our school. He'd even charmed the pants off of our classroom trainer, but he didn't learn his stuff. He was, in fact, completely incompetent.

We asked Palmer to go back through our sales school. He promised us he'd do his homework and learn the products and the pitch. After another two weeks in class, I took Palmer back out into the field. This time, he agreed to make some approaches and give a few presentations. It was a hot mess! Palmer was all over the place. His approach and pitch were incoherent. During one of his attempts, after he completely lost his way (and the prospect's attention), he glanced over at me as if to ask, "Can you please bail me out?"

It wasn't that he was shy or call reluctant. Palmer loved to talk to people. He didn't seem lazy; he was always willing to show up on time with a positive attitude. It wasn't that he couldn't get people to listen to him. He was extremely affable. Palmer was simply unwilling, or unable to absorb and apply the necessary skill sets needed to make a living in sales. We actually gave him one more chance to learn his core competencies before we terminated him.

Palmer was a perfect example of someone who was extremely incompetent. He came across as the brightest guy in the training room while enjoying the free doughnuts and coffee, but nothing intelligent came out of his mouth when he stepped in front of a prospect.

Okay, you say, Palmer was a goof-off; a slick guy who thought he could make it based on his gift of gab. He didn't want to put in the hours to learn, but what if you aren't willfully negligent, like Palmer? What if the resources to become competent aren't available to you?

As an example of that, I accepted a position at a fledging, personal computer service firm in the late 1980s. A person I'll refer to as Robert recruited me. The industry was emerging, and although I had very little technical knowledge of the personal computer industry, I sensed that the business was going to explode, so I took the position as sales manager. Sales is sales, right? I reported directly to Robert, who was the CEO and was dependent on him for support. That's where my problems started.

Robert was a whiz—he was a CPA by trade—but had become an expert on the PC industry and had carved out a great little business model that was centered on providing prepaid contract services to small businesses that had an abundance of personal computers and local area networks (LANS). Robert told me not to worry about my lack of knowledge; he said, "I'll teach you all you need to know."

Upon taking the position, I met the salespeople that Robert had hired.

They were running around, making sales sporadically and accidentally. His turnover of salespeople had been over 100 percent during the previous two-year period. The existing sales team had no real strategy and limited knowledge of our own levels of service. They weren't even 100 percent sure how to properly quote our plans. I realized I'd need to quickly absorb as much as I could about the newly emerging industry. I'd also need to know why a business owner would want to meet with us in the first place, and how our core services could be properly presented to solve their problems.

I approached Robert and tried to get on his calendar. I told him that I needed some focused time so that I could extract the specific knowledge needed to make the sales process work. His response was, and I'm quoting him exactly, "I hired you because you know how to sell and train people to sell. Go do your job and don't bother me with any of the gory details."

Robert might have been a smart guy, but he had no clue what components make up a successful sales process and culture. Worse, he wasn't open to learning what those pieces were. This job represented the shortest tenure I've experienced with any company I've worked with, just shy of ninety days! I had no choice but to leave. I was incompetent; I was managing people equally as incompetent; and there were no resources on the horizon that would allow us to become competent. I couldn't, in good conscious, hire people and throw them out to the wolves to fail. In addition, I couldn't sell programs to clients not knowing if I was even representing them accurately.

In the end, it won't matter whether you are unwilling to learn the core Competencies or if the organization you are part of doesn't teach them to you. Either way, a key piece of the equation will be missing, and the result will be the same: you'll crash and burn.

In Part II we explore the importance of the hard-wired Competencies that comprise the most straightforward part of The CAP Equation©. Your specific set of core proficiencies are made up of components that can usually be learned online, from written training guides, or from your organizational trainer in the classroom or in the field.

We will walk you through the key Competencies needed starting with an understanding of your industry, market, and products. Then we will challenge you to develop your unique selling propositions, leads, and appointment-generating skills. We'll break down the essential elements that make up the presentation and discuss closing and overcoming objections. We even teach you to make the sale after the sale and ask for referrals.

Throughout this book, I'm going to suggest that you visit our CAP Equation© website to obtain various resources. Below is the link and QR code that will take you to our home site and resources page that will support you in applying the content in this book.

www.thecapequation.com/resources/

Free Resources

To Support This Book

When you use the link or QR code you will be able to register when prompted with your name and email address. You will then be able to access valuable PDF downloads at no cost that will support your discovery of the three main components of The CAP Equation©.

In the last part of this book we are also going to direct you to download this worksheet. We will suggest that you carefully rate yourself using this tool. The completed worksheet will comprise your CAP Score© for the basic components needed to survive and thrive in sales.

It all starts with some solid Competencies and that's what this next part of the book will be dedicated to. This is where you will begin to do the work, but more than that, I'm going to ask you to *honor* the work. What I mean by "honor" is that I want you to respect the work to the extent that you'll want to become the best at it that you can possibly become.

The 20 percent practice this. They want to be the best prospector, presenter, closer, and so on. They want to become an ultimate professional. For them, this desire to excel goes beyond earning commissions. Oh, don't get me wrong; they want to earn a great deal of money, but they have tremendous pride; they want to be recognized as the best at what they do.

The 80 percent, guys like Rick Palmer? Not so much. They do some of the work, what seems convenient to them, but they're not completely dedicated. They're certainly not focused on the *quality* of the work. I guess you can say they go through the motions and then ask, "When's the money coming?"

Most of us go into commission sales to create independence and freedom. The cost of that is your willingness to put in the time and your inclination to continue paying dues to stay on top. Let's begin the hard work on the way to your independence and freedom.

CHAPTER 6

The Landscape

Industry, Market and
Core Product Knowledge

"Be curious always! For knowledge will not
acquire you; you must acquire it."

— **BERTRAND RUSSELL,** British philosopher and logician

The Competencies we recommend you identify and learn are broken into subsets—logical groups. In this chapter, we discuss industry knowledge—your geographic and target-market knowledge and that of your core products. We call this the "landscape." Let's dive a little deeper into each one of these Competencies individually.

INDUSTRY KNOWLEDGE

Why should you learn about your industry? If you have an understanding of things outside of the bubble you're in, you'll be able to thoughtfully respond to concerns or objections that might not have been discussed in your initial training. For example, if you know a little about your competition, you can intelligently compare and contrast versus being caught off guard when your prospect references them.

There's no shortage of blogs, newsletters, websites, LinkedIn groups, Facebook pages, trade or industry associations, breakfast and lunch meetings, and so on. I'm not suggesting that you do all of this at once, spend a great deal of money, or do research during your prime selling hours. In fact, I suggest you start with resources that are free and easily accessible using your nonprime time.

GEOGRAPHIC MARKET

Learn about the opportunities in your local geographic market and go as deep as you can in that local market. If you have an open market, then, by all means, select a defined geographic area to focus on. It's always more effective to have a focused geographical area versus a shotgun approach. In the Pipeline section of this book, we teach you that it's always better to call on one hundred prospects five times versus calling on five hundred leads one time. If you have a tighter, more defined geography, it is easier to do this. Also, when you concentrate your efforts in a defined area, there is less wear and tear on you and your car. You are also avoiding excess windshield time.

TARGET MARKET

Every company or organization has a target market to sell to. This is the person or company that is more receptive than others to your products and services. Another word that comes to mind is *profile*; your target has a definite profile. It's your job to figure out what that specific, target-market sector or person looks like and smells like as fast as you can. I'm also going to challenge you to learn which part of your market *turns* the quickest. Another terminology used for this is a *short-cycle sale.*

When you're identifying your ideal prospect, ask the following questions:

- What does your perfect customer *really* want?
- How can your product or service solve their problem?
- What factors motivate their buying decisions?
- Why do your clients choose you over your competitors?

Ask your hierarchy what type of prospect can be closed quickly and which ones require more time. This can be critical because we are assuming your gig requires *ramp-up time* and your reserves are most likely limited. This lone factor can make the difference between you sticking and staying or crashing and burning.

CORE PRODUCTS AND SERVICES

It's critical to know what products and services in your line are *core* versus noncore. Typically, 80 percent of your sales will be made up of only 20 percent of your product line. (There goes Mr. Pareto's principle again!)

You've got to get to the core and figure out what is going to feed you. I must warn you, the organization will probably train the heck out of you. I am sure they'll want you to know every little detail about every little product, service, or program that they offer. As controversial as this may sound, the hard facts suggest that many of those products and details may not make up the core offerings that your target actually buys. Hence, figure out what the *core* is (what people want and why they will listen to you) and focus on learning those products, services and programs inside and out. This makes more sense than trying to learn and sell each and every product or service in your line.

I'm not suggesting that the organization you're part of is derelict for trying to transfer all their product knowledge to you at once. They want to teach you everything. That's a good thing, but the truth is, you won't need that entire dump of information to succeed. In fact, struggling to learn and sell every product or service you have may endanger your ultimate goal of survival.

Focus on the vital few products and services in your line, the 20 percent that will make up 80 percent of your total sales. Your job is to survive, not learn each and every one of your products and selling points. If we agree that you need to slowly learn about your industry—to get outside of your company's bubble—to be better prepared and sound more enlightened, then do this on your nonprime-selling time.

I've hopefully sold you on identifying your core geographic and demographic markets. This will laser focus you on whom you need to be placing in your Pipeline and calling on. The last, strong suggestion that I've made in this chapter is that you need to figure out what products and services are core to your survival and focus on learning them first.

It's time to move on to the next set of Competencies. We are going to ask you to open your mouth and start filling up your calendar.

CHAPTER 7

Open Your Mouth

Communication Skills and
Unique Selling Propositions

"Communication—the human connection—
is the key to personal and career success."

—**PAUL J. MEYER,** Founder,
Success Motivation Institute

This second subset of Competencies discusses the essentials you'll need to begin successfully communicating your message to your target audience. In this chapter, we cover general communication skills and the development of your unique selling proposition. Let's dive in.

GENERAL COMMUNICATION SKILLS

When I began in outside sales, I was a bit shy; you could even describe me as awkward. I wasn't the guy who would be the center of attention at a gathering. I'd be the guy with my back up against the wall, waiting for someone to approach me. While being in a group was uncomfortable, being face-to-face with someone was even a little more painful.

By the time I left my very first job at the car lot and made my way to Penn Life, I knew I needed to develop some game in this area of communication skills. I began reading voraciously. Among the first three books I read was Dale Carnegie's *How to Win Friends and Influence People*. This book was a godsend for me, a foundational piece of my initial survival. It shaped the way I learned to communicate. When we get to the Attitudes section of this book, I'll explain how important reading was for me as I began my career in sales. Hopefully, I will impress you with the importance of self-educating as I tell the story that led me to a career of study about our craft.

I fear that many younger people involved in sales today have challenges communicating professionally. I think there might be societally rooted causes for this. Many people under the age of thirty might have never known a life without a multitude of technology-driven communication options. For example, when I completed my daily production activities at Penn Life, I would pick up the phone and call my manager. The dozen or so salespeople on his team were instructed to contact him between 5:00 p.m.–6:30 p.m. We were asked to keep it short and give him the number of approaches we made, followed by the number of full presentations given, and then, finally, the number of units of sale we made.

Good, bad, or ugly, we had to call in each evening and report our numbers. We had to have a brief, two-way conversation about the day—articulate what went well and what didn't, answer questions, and accept constructive criticism. I assure you, it was always easier to call my manager when I had a good day. It was usually a shorter call because I was anxious to celebrate with a cold beer. The conversations were more tedious and typically longer when the day didn't go well.

If you think about it, in today's world, that same type of interaction would probably occur digitally. We'd open our customer-relationship-manager app on our mobile device and punch in the numbers. Our sales manager or hierarchy might or might not see it that night because of the crush of digital information they have to process. It may take them a few days to aggregate the numbers and then shoot over an e-mail or text congratulating us, encouraging us, or terminating us. Regardless, what used to be a human conversation with real humanoid input is now merely an impersonal, digital string. Gone is the fine art of connection, the fine art of conversation.

It is my belief that, as a society, we are losing opportunities to truly connect and communicate. That muscle is suffering atrophy. So, whether you are sixty years old or twenty-two years old, let's pick up our heads, put down our mobile devices and tablets, and start having conversations that are engaging, conversations that matter. Let's start rebuilding these critical muscles.

I am heavily suggesting you engage in practices that assist you in improving both your one-on-one interaction skills as well as your group communication proficiencies. Here are some thoughts and ideas to get you started on your journey to being a great communicator:

- **Read**–Begin with *How to Win Friends and Influence People*. This book is a timeless classic and can be found on our recommended reading list at:

www.thecapequation.com/resources/

- **Attend**–Join a networking group that will ask you to present what you do or sell. In a networking group, you will be obliged to improve your interpersonal and group-speaking skills, but it's a safe place to do so, because most of the people there won't be direct targets of yours. It doesn't matter all that much if you trip over a few words. If you are scared to death of this idea, then you need to join Toastmasters and seriously hone your public speaking skills. This is a very safe place to work on all facets of your communication skills.

- **Tryout**–Start to alter the way your conversations with people go.

Instead of talking about yourself, make the conversation about them. Script out three to five open-ended questions (an open-ended question is a question that can't be answered with a "yes" or a "no"), and then develop a few follow-up questions. Focus on learning as much as you can about them the first time you meet them. If you wind them up, you can sit back and let them talk about themselves for a while. When you're done, they will think you are the smartest and coolest person in the room and they will love you.

Make a conscious effort to become a skilled communicator. It will be an extremely marketable skill in the future based on the digital habits of our younger generations.

UNIQUE SELLING PROPOSITION (USP)
(AKA "Elevator Pitch")

A *unique selling proposition* (USP) is the bedrock of how you present your personal brand, your organization, and your offerings. Your USP can and should also be condensed into an abridged version of what you do, how you do it, why it's unique, and how it benefits people.

A USP is also referred to as an "elevator pitch" that describes this shortened version. The term comes from the thought that a well-crafted—but abbreviated—USP can be delivered to a person you meet in an elevator as you are riding between the eighth floor and the lobby. It's a very handy skill and should be one of the first things you script for yourself, personalize, and commit to memory. It will be used whenever you have an opportunity to network, create a direct or indirect lead, or any other time you're put on the spot and asked to describe what you do.

Unique selling propositions aren't new; they've been used in successful advertising campaigns since the early 1940s. Advertisers create unique propositions that convince customers to switch brands; they create a *differentiation* between themselves and their competition. Theodore Levitt, a professor at Harvard Business School, stated that, "Differentiation is one of the most important strategic and tactical activities in which companies must constantly engage." Levitt's statement is important because you have to stand apart in a jam-packed marketplace; it helps if your brand has a trait that is worth remembering.

You will have to connect your brand with a clear benefit claim. Consumers don't want to buy your products—they want your products to solve their problems. Your USP, or elevator pitch, should make your business seem irresistible; however, the challenge I see with most people's elevator pitch is that they'll answer the question, "So, what do you do?" too literally. They will introduce what they do in such a way that it doesn't engage or provoke thought. Monotonous answers don't prolong the conversation productively. Here's an example using my trade. (Author, speaker and sales coach) Let's suppose somebody asks me what I do. I could say: "I write books on sales, speak nationally and also coach salespeople."

This would be a truthful and forthright answer, but wouldn't be a response that furthered my objectives. The person listening is likely to answer, "Oh, that's nice."

Let's change this up a little and walk through the pieces of a well-crafted and abridged elevator pitch. Again, I will use the business I'm in now as an example. (Please note that everything in parentheses in the following list can be altered to suit the particulars of your programs)

Our (coaching and training programs) are:

- **For** (professional salespeople and sales leaders)
- **Who** (have a burning desire to jump to the next level of income but need solid guidance in order to get there)
- (The CAP Equation©)
- **Is** (a set of proven methods and resources)
- **That** (produce real results for sales professionals)
- **Unlike** (other programs that may offer complex theories that haven't been proven out in the real world)
- **We are** (one of the few sales and leadership training organizations led only by people with vast field experience)

Do you see the difference? There is a clear benefit claim. I think you can see that it's pretty easy to craft an elevator pitch once you use this type of template. This model provides you with a way to communicate your offer in a concise and effective way.

When you find yourself suddenly face-to-face with a person who has a direct or indirect center of influence and can help you in your career, you need to be ready to engage that individual and create a *differentiation* in this person's mind between you and all others in your industry. These are golden opportunities that can propel your career forward. Work up your USP, your elevator pitch. Get good at it.

CHAPTER 8

Prospecting for Gold

*Raw Leads, Conversion and
Driving Appointments*

*"Sales are contingent upon the attitude of the
salesman—not the attitude of the prospect."*

— **W. CLEMENT STONE**, author,
founder of Combined Insurance Co.

In this set of Competencies we will focus on the basics of lead creation, lead conversion, and appointment setting. You will need to have your *A* game in this area if you expect to successfully gain an audience with decision makers. These are the people who can say, "yes" to your product, service, or offering.

Some aspects of these proficiencies cross over and are discussed as part of our section on Pipeline practices; however, let's explore a few points that can be primarily considered Competencies—skills you will need to deliberately develop. Let's first discuss the collection of raw leads and their immediate handling.

RAW-LEAD GENERATION (× 2 Philosophy)

This is an extremely straightforward proficiency that demands that you gather and load raw leads into your Pipeline in great volume. In fact, regardless of how many leads your organization or upline tells you to have, you should *double* that number. We want you to be so confident in the condition of your Pipeline that you can't wait to dig into it and start calling on the leads. The picture I have in my mind for this practice is that your Pipeline is so full that it is overflowing, spitting out excess raw leads and money all over the floor.

The reason I teach salespeople to have *twice* the raw leads they'll ever need in their funnel is so that meeting their income goals becomes easier in their minds. Think about it; if you had twice the number of leads in your pipeline right now, how would it make you feel? More confident about your near term activity levels? Would it free you up to want to tear through the leads faster?

I know, this seems like some kind of Jedi mind trick, but it really works. When my mentor asked me to double the number of raw leads in my pipeline in 1982 my commission flow began to dramatically increase almost immediately...and I hadn't become any more skillful in any other area.

Try this!

MULTIPLE-LEAD SOURCES (All Spigots)

We also want you to identify every raw-lead source possible, regardless of how effective you think it might be. When getting started, your job is to fill the lead funnel and to keep it full. There will be a time to become more selective about where your leads come from, but that isn't productive during your first six to nine months. Let's not get too meticulous with this process. Volume is king up front. Turn on *all* lead sources you can find.

Target Lead Types
(Low-Hanging Fruit and Short-Cycle Sales)

After your raw leads are loaded in your funnel, we want you to begin to identify the most targeted of those leads. By "targeted," we're referring to the low-hanging fruit. By "low-hanging fruit," we mean those prospects that are most likely to buy your products or subscribe to your programs based on their industry or profile. Low hanging fruit can also describe leads that will convert into your highest return-on-investment (ROI) clients, those that are easy to close and don't require a great deal of service after the sale.

In addition to identifying targeted leads that are most prone to do business with you, it is also important that you start to identify leads that may be *short-cycle sales*. A short-cycle sale is one that closes quickly. These types of prospects don't take multiple meetings with various levels of decision makers to consummate.

Why is identifying and targeting short-cycle sales so important? If you are new in sales, we are assuming that you have limited funds to use during your ramp-up period; hence, you will need to get momentum working in your favor. Momentum can only work in your favor if your lead and prospecting strategies support identifying willing buyers who can close fast.

One dangerous inclination some new salespeople have is chasing the *big* deal. We call this faulty practice "chasing elephants." Conversely, we teach new salespeople to look for short-cycle sales—smaller cases that close quickly and easily. We call this practice "shooting rabbits." The logic is hopefully clear to you. If people only chase big deals, they can easily run out of time and money while waiting for them to close. However, if they are hunting down and closing a lot of small deals, they are keeping food on the table and also building momentum. Go shoot a lot of rabbits!

SELL THE APPOINTMENT

When you are ready to pick up the phone or cold call in person please make sure you are working from a proven script. Your organizational trainer should be able to supply you with a proven track to run on. The trainer should be able to teach you how to interest a prospect in meeting with you without you having to dump your whole load of data on them.

You've got to sell the appointment—the time to meet—to your prospect, not all the other stuff. Your prospect or gatekeeper will be great at baiting you into a deeper conversation on the phone. They'll ask, "Can you tell me a little more about your program?" You can get sucked into that, but that simply won't help you get a face-to-face appointment with them. They'll sometimes ask, "Can you send me a brochure?" When asked this, I would politely answer, "My company has spent a great deal of time and money creating an all-inclusive, multimedia, interactive brochure that answers all your questions, and that brochure is *me*. So is Tuesday or Wednesday better for you this week?"

If you are new in your position, you won't have the depth of knowledge that you will eventually have. Hopefully, your trainer will give you just enough knowledge to set appointments, and that's probably what you'll do...set appointments. But then you'll learn more about your programs and you'll be tempted to sell over the phone. You'll sell concepts, products, services, features, benefits or whatever else you've learned. You'll begin *data dumping*. You'll sell everything but the appointment. As a result, your appointment-setting ratio will crash. We call this the *curse of knowledge*. *Sell the appointment, the time to get together,* and nothing else.

RICHES IN *NICHES*

One other strategy you might want to employ is that of niche marketing and prospecting. We've seen a lot of salespeople discover a market niche for themselves. They become involved in the inner circle of an industry and begin receiving referrals. They *warm-call* versus cold-call. Ask yourself a few questions as you formulate your prospecting plans:

- What *type/size* of prospect am I comfortable talking with?
- Do I have a prior industry *background* that can be exploited?
- What industry niches exist in volume in my *geographical area*?
- Can I network my way into an industry *inner circle*?

Find a niche and *go deep*; you will turbo charge your production.

WORK SMART (CALL DURING *OFF-PEAK* HOURS)

One of the most common questions I'm asked regarding B2B prospecting and appointment setting is, "How can I get *past* the gatekeeper?" This is a good question, but there's a better question. The smarter question would be, "How can I *eliminate* the gatekeeper?" I have the answer. There's an easy way to do this in B2B prospecting. You simply need to call on your target decision maker at a time when the gatekeeper isn't there!

If you drive into the parking lot of your prospect at 7:30 a.m., what kind of cars will be sitting in that lot? You will see a brand new truck with *Smith Brother's Commercial Plumbing* painted on the side, or you might see a Mercedes or a Lexus. If you drive into that same parking lot at 6:15 p.m. in the evening, what cars will you see? That's right, the same truck or Lexus.

The gatekeepers arrive one minute before they have to punch the clock. If starting time is 8:30 a.m., and you call on the account at 7:45 a.m., your path is clear. When the whistle blows at 5:00 p.m., there is a mass exodus of employees. By 5:01 p.m., the rank and file are already burning rubber out of the parking lot. Again, no gatekeeper; your path is clear!

Obviously, we are imploring you to work smart along with working hard. If you make field or phone calls during *off peak* hours, you often take the gatekeeper out of the equation. If you practice this strategy, your appointment-setting volume will increase. If you plan your schedule so that you can start early or call on businesses late, it will pay dividends. Also, you'll stand apart in your prospect's mind—they will see you as a committed entrepreneur, just like them.

USE A CUSTOMER-RELATIONSHIP-MANAGEMENT TOOL (CRM) (Automate)

Most top producers use some type of customer-relationship-management program (CRM). This is usually in the form of an online, cloud-based program. A CRM program will manage your leads and other pertinent data while automating the work. We will discuss this subject in detail in the Pipeline section of this book; however, we want you to begin thinking about what system you'll use to manage and track your leads. Your objectives should be to eliminate all business cards, lead sheets with scribbles, hard-copy files, and random sticky notes that wind up on your desk. I'm not certain how you can manage one hundred leads, let alone five hundred, if you don't go digital, using a CRM.

KNOW WHEN TO FOLD 'EM

I get asked this question a lot: "When should I stop calling on a lead?" The other question we are asked frequently is: "How often should I call the lead?" Let me answer the second question first. I've always recommended the *one voicemail per week* rule if you are using the phone. I believe that if you are calling on prospects in person, you can drop in on them twice in a week's time without being an annoyance.

Let me now address the second question—it's straightforward: you should follow up with your prospect until there isn't a reason to anymore. Let me expand on this. Most salespeople call on leads endlessly, for weeks, months, years, just trying to get the initial appointment. I, and others like me, don't have that brand of patience. I will ask them for a face-to-face meeting three times. If over some reasonable period of time with three *asks,* the answer is still "no," I'm okay tossing the lead in the trash. I'd much rather call on a few new fresh leads. Pros know when to hold leads and also know when to fold 'em. You must have a *compelling* reason to continue following up with a lead. If you've asked for an appointment three times, it's probably time to move on. It's better for your psyche.

Go *Warm* (As Soon as You Can)

We began to build on this earlier in this chapter when we suggested that you network into *niches*. We also cover this topic in great detail in the final chapter on Competencies. Make no mistake, the best way to prospect has always been, and always will be, to go *warm*. We encourage you to build and implement a *referral* system as soon as you can.

Know Your Appointment-Conversion Ratio (Ask for Help if Needed)

We cover this subject in more depth as part of our section on Pipeline practices; however, as you are doing the prospecting work, it's critical for you to know exactly what your conversion ratio of prospects to appointments is. Knowing your conversion ratios allows you to schedule enough time for prospecting and also tells you if you are above or below your local organization's standards. If you are converting leads to appointments at a rate that is below standard, please yell for help. This is one of those make-it-or-break-it metrics.

Put the Pressure on the Numbers

This is such a critical concept, and we will certainly revisit and apply it several more times. The bottom line on applying this concept to appointment setting is that you have to build a prospecting *system* that you can trust. When you've refined your skill set and determined what your conversion ratio is, then you have to *trust* your system and continue to crank that wheel.

Never Stop Prospecting

There are only two reasons salespeople *stop* prospecting: they either have too *much* success or too *little*. They either freak out, get scared that all that business is pouring in and that they won't be able to handle it; or they have poor results and their emotional gas tank becomes empty. Either one of these reasons is not a good-enough reason to stop prospecting. If you have too much success, then simply keep prospecting and ask for help. If you are having too little success...yeah, then keep prospecting, and—you guessed it—ask for help.

All sales professionals know that when you stop or slow your prospecting machine, you'll pay a *deferred* penalty. Somewhere between sixty and ninety days after you stop prospecting, you will be out of business. Your Pipeline will be empty. This is a predictable death spiral.

Pros don't stop prospecting. They do develop warm-lead sources and referral systems. They begin to work *warm* leads close to 50 percent of the time beginning their second year. They can do this because they began to build out networking and referral systems during their first six to nine months.

CYCLE THROUGH SELECTED LEADS QUICKLY, X2, X3...

True sales professionals know that it's better to call on one hundred leads five times versus five hundred leads one time. Have you heard that one before? They know that most prospects, especially key executives or business owners, are insanely busy, but if their prospect sees that they're diligent in the follow-up process, they are more likely to respect that and grant the appointment. In addition, many of us are pounded by input, and only respond when we hear a message three to five times. You want to be on their minds...in their faces. During a typical prospecting cycle, make your plan to call on your selected leads at least *twice*, if not *three* times.

Bottom line, if we agree that there's always going to be some *pain* when prospecting, wouldn't it be wise to *front-load* it...get it out of the way fast? Like the saying goes, "When you're running through *hell*, keep running."

Let's end this chapter by touching on what your rules should be for a prospecting calendar.

A *FULL* PROSPECTING AND APPOINTMENT CALENDAR

Continuing the theme we touched on in chapter 4, I will mention it again (as it pertains to prospecting and appointments): you must commit to having a calendar full of appointments, especially in your first six to nine months. All pros settle on this, deciding up-front in their careers, that having a full appointment load is the only way they'll be able to meet their income goals.

If you are new in sales or trying to get to the next level, the one thing that will get you there the fastest is generating qualified appointments in volume. To accomplish this, you'll have to be purposeful and it will have to be preplanned and calendar driven. The top 20 percent live by the following disciplines:

- They identify prospecting priorities and *ink* them in the calendar
- They look for *holes* in the calendar and *fill* them
- They select specific leads to work and *work them*
- They prospect for hours at a time, *head down*, no distractions

Pros place intense focus on completing their planned prospecting sessions. For example, they set goals, such as making one hundred calls, walking into thirty doors, or canvassing for four hours. Then, after that clear objective is set, they focus on completing it and nothing else. They don't focus on any of the micro results inside of the overall task. There is no emotion expended; only analysis after the session is over.

Once pros set their prospecting and appointment calendars, they forget about it and they jump into the "zone." They can do this because their calendar is *airtight*. When they are certain their calendars are tight, they switch on their autopilots and become consciously *unconscious*.

On the contrary, the other 80 percent don't make prospecting and appointment setting a hard-wired activity. To them, it's something they'll do when they *get around to it,* and that's if they get around to it at all. The seeds of their failure are sewn right there and then.

Once you get these lead generating, lead-conversion, and appointment-setting Competencies committed to *habit*, it can be fun. From early on in my career, I decided to make a big game out of this area to keep it fun. I removed emotion from the equation. We teach you how to do this as we go deeper into the mental elements of The CAP Equation©. But next we'll discuss building your engaging presentation.

CHAPTER 9

Engage

Building Your Presentation

"Keep the customer actively involved throughout your presentation, and watch your results improve."

—HARVEY MACKAY,
entrepreneur, author

After you've begun to fill your calendar with qualified appointments, it is of paramount importance that you become proficient in the Competencies that put you in a position to get paid. When you have the opportunity to deliver your message, it must be in the form of an engaging presentation. We examine what elements comprise a solid presentation in this chapter.

PRESENTATION SKILLS

Sales organizations are all over the board on what they teach regarding presentations. Some have a *canned pitch* they ask you to learn. Some have a *track*, but allow for variance. Some presentations border on *data dumps* with little or no engagement, while others are nothing but engaging, to the point that your prospects feel interrogated when you get finished with them.

Regardless of what they teach, you should learn their program. Don't argue with them, don't question it, and don't fight it. Just learn it! Learn their pitch verbatim—memorize it as your *default* program. You can always tweak things later, and you probably will.

Here's my logic on this point: Your company's training protocols can't be that bad. If they are that horrendous, then you made a horrible selection of a company to work with. Assuming your organization's training program is tolerable, then learn their pitch, learn it well—know it in your sleep and begin to use it. It will give you a default method of presenting so you aren't all over the place and you're doing the same thing every time.

Doing the same thing each time accomplishes two things: First, it removes confusion. In sales, confusion will always lead to a slowdown in activity, which always leads to a death spiral. When you know what you're going to say and ask each time you sit with a prospect, it frees your mind to focus on your closing sequence and also allows you to focus on the numbers.

The other advantage of doing the same thing every time is that your overall block of results can be analyzed; hence, you can be coached. If your trainer doesn't know what you are saying from call to call, your trainer can't help you. You won't be able to tell the doctor where it hurts, and the doctor won't be able to prescribe a solution. Again, you can always modify your presentation once you have some experience under your belt. After six to nine months of experience, you can confer with peers who are knocking it out of the park. You can ask them if or how they've modified the standard pitch.

Let's join the conversation that's in your prospects' heads and discuss the five basic buying decisions that they always make regardless of what you are selling.

The Five Basic Buying Decisions

1. *You*

One of the first lessons I was ever taught in sales is that they don't buy from you unless they trust and like you. It is also critical to note that prospects begin judging you when you walk in the door. They start sizing you up immediately. It stands to reason that if you want your prospects to like you, you must like them first. Sometimes I think we form mental barriers in our minds with regard to our prospects and targets. We almost create an *"us against them"* thing. Let's erase that barrier. Here are five reasons you might want to like your prospects:

- **Prospects buy things:** Their purchasing dollars become your commission dollars. Their problems help shade your solutions. They are the *only* reasons you exist.

- **Customers know things and people you don't:** Your customers are knee-deep in an industry you want to serve. They have relationships and contacts in that business. They have an insider's viewpoint of how things work.

- **Your prospects begin each day wanting to do their best:** In this respect, they're exactly like you. They get up, have their coffee, and head out the door or to their computer, intending to be the best they can be. They don't start the day intending to make a lot of mistakes or do a bad job.

- **Some customers are smarter than others:** These folks might be your early adopters. They also might be more challenging. When you're dealing with customers who aren't quite so quick or competent, it's your opportunity to help them succeed.

- **Prospects are human:** They have good days and bad. They have budgets and pressures that they have to meet. Sometimes their well-intended decisions get reversed, and sometimes they do make mistakes. Anticipate that these events will occur and do some scenario planning to protect your own objectives.

2. *Your Company or Organization*

The second buying decision your prospects have to make are relevant to your company or organization. They'll learn of your company's reputation and evaluate if your organization is a good match for theirs. You will have to figure out if their perception of your organization is consistent with what your company really is. They will be asking if your organization is a thought leader within the industry you represent.

3. *The Solution (Not Your Product)*

They will have to decide if the solution you're presenting is viable and if they will improve their position personally (WIIFM—what's in it for me?) and if these solutions create a new and better reality for their family or organization. They will also have to feel an emotional connection to these results for the sale to move forward. Buyers rarely buy on logic; they make decisions based on emotion and justify with logic.

4. *Price, Cost, or Cost of Change*

There are two types of cost decisions that might exist: direct costs and indirect costs. Regardless of what program you are offering, even if there is no direct cost to the decision maker, your prospect will always perceive there's a cost. Sometimes it's simply an administrative cost; sometimes it's the cost of change—the "pain factor" of changing something they've been doing a long time. In other words, if they buy today, then they must do things differently tomorrow. The "cost of change" has to be addressed in some manner.

5. *When to Buy*

When to buy is the last of the five buying decisions. It's important to understand that, in a typical prospect's mind, it's easier to not make a decision versus making a wrong one. In the buyer's mind, putting off the decision ensures that a mistake isn't made. Urgency isn't a lever for you until you engage the decision maker *emotionally* in the sale.

These are the five buying decisions that *all* prospects have to make during your time with them, and they generally make those decisions in the order presented. What we'll discuss next are the ten elements that you need to practice during your presentation process. These elements will help you prepare for the presentation and address the buying decisions in the body of the presentation.

THE TEN ELEMENTS OF A PRESENTATION

1. Pre-presentation Preparation

This is your homework. We are suggesting that you learn all you can about your prospects through their website, LinkedIn, Facebook, and so on. Never ask them a question you could've learned the answer to using a Google search. After you've learned a little about them, you should draft a few, best questions you'll ask them to break the ice.

2. Call Objective and Readiness

Pre-set your commitment objective for the call based on what you know about them. For example, if you know that all decision makers will be present at the meeting, and you have a product or service that can be sold on a one-call basis, then your commitment objective should be to close on the first call. However, if you're aware that people in the decision-making loop won't be at the meeting, then your commitment objective becomes to secure a second meeting with all of the pertinent parties. If the second scenario exists, then be sure that you have identified at least two calendar options and be ready to pivot.

3. Vital Connection to Prospect

You know the old saying: "you only one get one chance to make a good first impression." This is the element of the presentation where you will connect to your prospect and make that good first impression. Before leaving your home, make sure you are dressed for success, arrive early, and by all means, be Switzerland—neutral. No discussion of politics or religion. Also, don't tell any bad jokes. Don't try to be funny; in fact, don't try to be anything you aren't.

This is where you can use those personal questions, the ones you drafted after researching your prospects and their company. You can inspire them to talk about their favorite subject—themselves. After this, the more they talk, the *smarter* you are, and the more they like you.

4. Engaging Discovery

The key to an engaging presentation lies in the questions you select and then ask. You must ask the right questions and even smarter follow-up questions, but at the same time, you have to be careful. Asking too many questions in a rapid-fire manner without being conscious of the flow of conversation can make your prospects feel like they are being interrogated. You must follow the flow of conversation and use your inventory of questions sparingly.

The organization you work with should have a list of questions that specifically apply to the products or services you offer. I would suggest you obtain that list and begin to craft your presentation selecting some of those questions. We have prepared a sample inventory of questions to get you started if your trainer, mentor, or organization doesn't have a list of best questions. Please go to the link below and pull down the inventory list of questions:

www.thecapequation.com/resources/

You will notice that the questions on our resource list are broken down by category. You might also notice a few questions that begin with, "How," "Would" and, "What would." These are big, open-ended questions and are killers to use as follow-up questions. Make sure you go to the link, download these questions and begin using them if you don't already have an inventory.

5. Mutual Agreement of Needs and Opportunities

I like to refer to this part of the presentation as gathering arrows. The "arrows" I'm referring to are the *needs* and *opportunities* arrows. In this part of the presentation, you will carefully understand your prospects' needs and then feed those needs back to your prospects. Your goal is to confirm these needs and then ask a "how would" or a "what would" question.

The payoff occurs when you don't *stop* at the first arrow (need) that you gather. You want to go as deep as you can while they're telling you what's important to them. Gather as many arrows as possible but don't begin shooting them back at your prospect or try to close them yet. Use great discipline to simply collect and store your ammo. These arrows will come in handy later when you are overcoming objections.

6. Positioning Your Organization

Hopefully, you have asked great questions, ones that helped you understand what's important to your prospects in the selection of a partner. They might have used words such as "caring" or "responsive." Write those key words down. When positioning your organization, model those words. Build those same trigger-words back into the description of your organization.

Hopefully, you are also positioning your organization as a *thought leader*. Most prospects love the idea of doing business with a cutting-edge organization or person. Demonstrate the differentiators of your organization. Connect your company's *culture* to theirs. In other words, make sure that you are selling them the type of company they would want to work with, partner with, or buy from.

7. Positioning Your Solution(s)

This is where you get to propose a big solution for your prospects. Most new salespeople want to push out a product or a specific feature of a product. Amateurs data dump, but that's not what works. What does drive the sale forward is to show them how the *features* of your program affect them (or their end consumer) positively; then you must establish how your solution creates a *new reality* for them personally.

> **Always remember, your prospect doesn't simply want to buy your product, they want your product to solve their problems.**

After you demonstrate how the features solve their problem and the solution creates a new reality, then you must connect them to the solution(s) *emotionally*. To accomplish this, you can ask an open-ended question and gain their buy-in. This can also be considered a trial close. Once you've pulled the lever of emotion, the sale will move forward. As we've stated, most people don't buy *now* simply based on logic; they buy based on emotion, then, they justify their decision based on logic and good business reasons.

8. *Trial Closing/Handling Objections*

I go much deeper on the subject of closing in the next part of this section; however, in summary, after you agree on needs and position your solutions, you're ready to use a trial close. Before you begin to use trial and assumptive closes, make sure you have at least *two arrows* ready. It is ideal to follow-up a positive response with an, "Is it okay?" type of question. For example: "Is it okay if I explain how we'd install this program?" or "Is it okay if I explain how we'd educate your staff?"

The two reasons you'll use a trial or assumptive close are as follows: First, to establish where you *stand* in respect to an actual sale. The trial or assumptive close is an easy way to establish your *ground position*. Secondly, a trial or assumptive close might uncover one or more specific objections that you've not answered in the body of the presentation. We have found that asking them permission to discuss one of the next steps in the process is an easy way to move into the area where the *real* selling begins.

9. *Creating Optimal Fulfillment Conditions*

In most sales processes, there is a secondary sale to be made. This is the sale that sets up the fulfillment conditions. This sale can be just as important as the initial sale, if not more so. The critical point here is to slow down and relax after the prospect says, "Yes." It's at this juncture that you want to tee yourself up with your ideal fulfillment conditions, which you want to happen next.

10. *Review the Call*

You have a golden opportunity after you complete each presentation. You have the chance to tear your work apart and ask the following questions:

- What went well?
- What didn't go so well?
- What will I never do again?

My suggestion is for you to do this at the very first opportunity so all of the details are fresh in your mind. This is such an important practice. Remember, we learn the most when things don't go well. This is the time to break down every presentation to determine if you addressed the five buying decisions and that each critical element of your presentation was solidly executed.

On the next page, we have included a sample matrix of the five buying decisions and the ten presentation elements. The matrix shows how each set of dynamics will line up with the other. We invite you to go to our website and download a PDF copy of this. It can be handy to review before a presentation to ensure you don't miss any of the elements on either side of the closing table. Please go to:

www.thecapequation.com/resources/

Okay. We have built a presentation that encompasses all of the critical elements. We have spoken to the five buying decisions, uncovered needs and opportunities and gotten our prospect to agree with them. Are you ready to close?

The FIVE Buying Decisions & TEN Presentation Elements

WWW.CAPequation.com

Buying Decisions	Presentation Elements	
Pregame	1	Research & Preparation
	2	Call Objectives & Readiness
	3	Vital Connection to Prospect
1. You	4	Engaging Discovery
	5	Mutual Agreement of Needs
2. Your Organization	6	Positioning Your Organization
3. The Solution	7	Positioning Your Solution
4. Cost		
5. When to Buy	8	Trial Closing/Handling Objections
Postgame	9	Creating Optimal Fulfillment Conditions
	10	Review the Call

CHAPTER 10

Trial Close and Listen

Identifying Prospect Responses

"I believe most salespeople need to be a little hard of hearing when the prospect says they are not interested."

—ZIG ZIGLAR

This might be hard for you to believe, but the vast majority of salespeople out there don't have a clue as how to close a sale. Most don't have at least three practiced methods of asking a prospect to buy. Most people that call themselves a professional salesperson give a decent presentation, and then freeze. A lot of them wait for the prospect to close themselves, or worse, they blurt out something like, "So, what do you think?" When the prospect responds with, "Let me think this over," the salesperson is relieved. At least they can tell their managers that they didn't get a

"No." Again, I know it's hard to believe, but the reality of it is that most salespeople are completely lost when it comes to closing, and they have no road map to help them get home.

In this chapter and the next, we will dedicate our time to examining what should occur as you transition from your engaging presentation to the closing process. In fact, in chapter 11 we are going to introduce a GPS device we call the CAP Closing Matrix©. We will teach you that the "closing process" is really more of a "closing sequence." It has definite transitions to be navigated and detours to be taken. You must process these in a particular order if you are going to get back onto the main highway and get home safely. Let's first, in this chapter, discuss the basic types of closes used and then we can define the four responses than can occur.

Closing Methods (Trial, Assumptive, and Direct)

I have always taught that *you have to have more ways of asking them to buy than they have of saying "No."* This simply means that when the prospect offers any response other than "Yes," your job of selling begins. While there are many types of closing methods you can employ, I'll give you examples of three of the most common.

Trial Close

This is usually a test close to determine whether your prospect is ready. It establishes your ground position. You would use this type of close after you've offered a solution and gained agreement that it filled a need that the prospect has. You will ask a trial-closing question that elicits a positive or confirming response. These big, open-ended, trial-closing questions can be used for a B2B sale, an individual sale, and also a recruiting scenario. They can sound like these examples:

- "It looks like you appreciate aspects of this program. How do you think implementing it here at ABC Company would benefit your organization?"

- "I know what your personal objectives are in regard to _____. How would this product help you accomplish those goals?"
- "Based on the direction you want to steer your future income, how instrumental would an opportunity like this be in getting you there?"

Of course, you can only use a trial close like these after you've conducted an engaging presentation, asked great questions, and gathered a few arrows. If so, you can take one of them out of your quiver, tie it to a trial close, and shoot it back to your prospect.

When you use a trial close—as with most other types of closes—be quiet, watch, and listen carefully for your prospect's response. A trial close works by putting the idea of closure into the person's mind. You will be able to tell by the response whether your prospect is ready to give you the order at that moment in time or is receptive to more direction and information.

Typically, if you've done everything right, and your prospect has engaged with you and given you summary agreements on needs and opportunities that would better or change the reality, your prospect will offer an extremely positive response to your trial-closing question. It can sound something like this:

> "I do like the basic concept of your program and these plans would benefit our rank-and-file employees more than anyone else here. But, I do have some concerns. I'm not sure enough of our employees will be interested to make this worth our while."

or...

> "I know I told you that our goal is to establish a secondary source of income so my wife can work from home, but we've never started a business or sold anything before...we're just not sure how successful we'd be."

These types of responses are great for you to receive because you've established your ground position. They are not ready to say "Yes" yet. There are concerns present and they are beginning to tell you about them. The prospect doesn't have enough information, and there is more work to be done.

At this time, you would ask clarifying questions about the prospect's concerns and then isolate them—ask the prospect if there are any *other* fears or concerns to discuss. If you quarantine the objection, then you can use the appropriate rebuttal that you have in your inventory, and then ask another trial close or go straight to a slightly stronger type of close—an *assumptive close.*

Assumptive Close

This is where you act *as if* the prospect has made a positive decision already. You turn the focus of the conversation toward the next step, such as how many they want, when they want it delivered, what size they need, and so on. Examples of what this might sound like are:

- "When should we schedule the installation?"
- "We discussed four different plans for your employees. Should we start the program this year with just our two most popular plans?"
- "You're probably wondering how we train and support our new distributors. Is it okay if I walk you through the sign-up and training process so you have a full understanding of it?"

The assumptive close works by using the assumption principle. Acting confidently, as if something is true, makes it difficult for the other person to deny this. To say you are wrong would be to cast himself or herself as an antisocial naysayer. This type of close is one of the most common closes used. Many other closes are variants of the assumptive close.

Direct/Logical Close

This is where you would use logic and reason to persuade. You'd show your prospect evidence that the product works well and that other customers were satisfied. You would leverage your irrefutable proof; explain reasonably why buying is the right choice. With care, you can construct a powerful argument that uses a traditional and proven structure for persuasion. For example:

> "We've gone through all your needs, and our program meets these well, right? And the price is good, true? Now, is there anything else that would stop you from buying today?"

This approach works simply by using reasoning that calls upon logic and science. As we are brought up in a social and educational system that defines science and reason to be correct, such an approach is powerfully persuasive, but also tends to be an *in-your-face*-type of close. This sort of close, by far, is *my least* favorite.

This is not a book that is all about how to close a sale; hence, it would be impossible for me to teach you all you'll eventually learn. However, on the topic of closing, I wanted to get you settled on what your main objective is. While many salespeople focus on the presentation itself as the closing tool, the presentation is simply a run-up to your closing questions, methods, and sequence. It's your job to arrive at a place where you can ask for the sale.

Let's now discuss your transition from an engaging presentation to the actual closing process and sequence. While conducting an engaging presentation and using trial or assumptive closes are the first steps in the process, the authentic game begins when the prospect offers an objection, condition, or stall. As we previously mentioned, when they say anything other than "Yes," the real selling begins.

IDENTIFYING OBJECTIONS, CONDITIONS, AND STALLS

When you have conducted a solid presentation, then asked for the sale using a trial or assumptive close, you have entered the closing zone. This is the juncture that separates the professionals from the amateurs in a big hurry. You can't and won't win them all. That's never been my goal and shouldn't be yours; however, your goal should be to win your fair share, and more importantly, know *why* you're winning or losing sales.

The only way you can do that is if you are not afraid to drive your prospect to an objection you know you have a rebuttal for.

If you are unable to accomplish this, your great presentation will be wasted, along with all the time leading up to it. When you ask for the sale using one or more of the closing questions you've learned, one of only four responses will result.

- Yes
- Objection
- Condition
- Stall

Of the four, I'm sure we all prefer the "Yes." However, an easy "Yes" occurs on the first close only a small percentage of the time. More often, prospects will turn your offer down, giving you one or more *objections*. At other times, they will show interest ("buying signals") but offer up a *condition*. A *condition* is a viable scenario or logistic that stands in the way of them buying. Often, we can collaborate with the buyer to find a solution and make the sales work.

In addition to "Yes", an objection, or a condition, there is also the dreaded *stall*. A *stall* in the process occurs when prospects tell us that they "like" what we've presented, but they want to "think it over" before they commit. A stall is a non-objection; something nonspecific that you can't rebut or have a discussion about. It is often the most difficult response for a new salesperson to handle.

Let's begin by discussing managing objections, conditions, and stalls the professional way. It is way too easy for a new salesperson to become confused, lost, or stranded at this juncture. The difference between the way pros and amateurs handle the closing sequence can be likened to each of them arriving at the same fork in the road and taking different paths. That's how I'd like you to think about this critical stage of the sales process. It's a fork in the road, and you can slow down, hit your GPS and allow it to guide you down the correct path, or you can take Yogi Berra's humorous advice: "If you come to a fork in the road, take it."

That philosophy might have worked for Yogi, but then again, he wasn't working on commission only; he had a salary. My point is you have to take a very disciplined set of skills into the closing zone. You need to know which fork is going to get you back to the main road—the closing road.

THE *WRONG* PATH

Think of the wrong path as a bumpy, rocky trail that eventually leads you to a dead end. Amateurs get *lost* when they near the end of their basic presentation. The only deals that they close are when their prospect closes themselves.

Unprepared salespeople tend to panic when a basic objection is offered. Amateurs also have a habit of arguing with a stall, or worse; they roll over and simply accept the nonspecific blow-off because a "maybe" is a *victory* to them. Amateurs often believe in repeatedly calling back on prospects that have given them a "maybe", never to identify and isolate what the true objection is. I think these same neophyte salespeople also believe in the tooth fairy. It's inevitable that a salesperson will run out of gas at some point on this bumpy path. Untrained salespeople simply don't know *where to go* after a "No", condition, or stall has resulted.

THE *CORRECT* PATH

The pros use GPSs. Their practiced closing process and sequence gives them a definite ground position. They are never lost. Pros know the *route* they're going to take from the moment they sit down with their prospects. When they come to a fork in the road, they *slow down* and use their maps.

Pros know that when their prospects don't say "Yes," there are only three other possible deviations from the main highway. They can identify the detours their prospects are taking immediately—all diversions are *familiar*. Professional closers know how to get back on the main road using their closing sequence. They don't panic; they gently guide their vehicles back onto their intended routes, which are not specific *places* as much as *results*.

If we've got you convinced that there is a finite number of responses that you have to be prepared for, and that there's definitely a right way to navigate them, then let's go deeper and define the four responses.

"Yes"

Hopefully, you know what a "Yes" sounds like. Unfortunately, there are some salespeople who don't. Sometimes a "Yes" is subtler than other times. Train your *ear* to pick up on when your prospect has given you the direction to move forward.

Objection ("No")

An objection is a rebuff for one or more *specific* reasons. They're not ready to say "Yes" *yet*. Make certain that this response isn't a *condition*.

Condition

A *condition* occurs when your prospect has genuine interest but conveys to you *valid logistic* or other scenarios that is prohibiting immediate forward movement. You must ask at least *two clarifying* questions to ensure that the response isn't an objection.

Stall

The *stall* is a nonspecific push back, a *nondecision* with no explicit cause given. It is usually expressed by your prospect asking for the time to "think about it," "kick it around," or some similar noncommittal response.

Now that we have heard them clearly and identified the only four responses that a prospect can offer, let's move on to the subject of driving to a definite result.

CHAPTER 11

The CAP Closing Matrix©

Driving to a Result Using a Closing Sequence

"Always be closing...that doesn't mean you're always closing the deal, but it does mean that you need to be always closing on the next step in the process."
—SHANE GIBSON, author, sales expert

While using trial and assumptive closes to trigger responses and establish your ground position is key, knowing where to go from there is everything. Being able to artfully navigate their response is the pay off. It's what gets you to a definite result quickly—which should always be your objective.

In the previous chapter we confirmed that your prospect's response must fit into one of the four categories listed. We pointed out that your job is to know what each response sounds like and then determine which category it fits into. In this chapter we will introduce The CAP Closing Matrix© and ask you to add this key instrument to your toolbox.

We will teach you how to use The CAP Closing Matrix© to effortlessly redirect your prospect back onto the main highway after he or she offers an objection, condition or stall. You will continue, using the closing sequence we teach and ask for the sale again. Remember, most deals aren't won until the third ask. Deals are won through a series of smaller trial and assumptive closes that are used throughout the sales presentation process.

Your good stuff has to be sprinkled throughout the presentation in the form of great questions and trial closes. If you haven't involved your customers in the conversation from the beginning, you aren't going to close them. Conversely, if you ask them to buy several times, in different ways, during the presentation, your odds of getting a "Yes" go way up.

Our CAP Closing Matrix© is a proven sequence that ensures that you will be able to use multiple closes during the process. With this sequence, you won't *lose* your prospects; they will be involved and engaged, and your closing rate will improve dramatically.

We have included an image of the CAP Closing Matrix© at the end of this chapter. You may want to take a look at it now, better yet, go to our home site and download a full size PDF so that you can follow along as you work through this chapter.

www.thecapequation.com/resources/

Let's revisit the four responses we discussed in chapter 10 and begin to develop a navigation process for each of them:

Handling a "Yes"

Hit your easy button and do the following:

- Congratulate your prospect on a great decision
- Resist the urge to continue selling (Stop talking!)
- Negotiate conditions you'll need to properly install your program
- Complete the paperwork

Slow down and solidify any conditions you will require to make the sign-up or installation of your product or program successful. This might require an additional calendar commitment from your prospect, and it's important that you gain a *strong commitment* for that on the spot. You can hook a fish, but if you don't bring the fish into your boat, you still go hungry.

Handling an Objection

As we previously defined, an *objection* sounds like "No", but it's more than just that. The prospects have given you one or more *specific* reasons why they're not ready to move forward. While they might not be ready to say "Yes" yet, they can often be closed if we follow the CAP Closing Matrix©. Oftentimes, they simply need more information. Let's take the following steps:

- Listen to the objection carefully. Ask as many *clarifying* questions as you need to understand it
- *Isolate* the objection. Make sure there are *no other* objections
- Use the *appropriate* rebuttal
- Close again

Handling Conditions

You have to be careful not to confuse a *condition* with an *objection*. Remember, a condition happens when your prospect is actually interested in moving forward with you, but there is some real scenario or challenge standing in the way. The condition could be that another decision maker is needed to approve the sale. The condition also could be a calendar concern, or it could be an administrative or system problem. Regardless, it is vitally important that you recognize that the prospect would like to move forward if this challenge can be overcome. When a condition arises, take the following steps:

- Ask *clarifying* questions and then *repeat back* the condition for confirmation

- Isolate it
- Make sure there are no additional *conditions* or *objections.*
- Set a new objective (a mutually, agreed-upon outcome)
- Set the next *meeting.*
- Gain a *summary commitment* (conditional approval)

Handling a Stall

New and even veteran salespeople crumble over this response. But it's actually one of the easiest responses to handle in the closing process. The reason it's so easy to navigate is that, in and of itself, the response has absolutely *no substance.* The response is baseless, and worse, it's a *lie,* and lies are generally easy to expose.

A stall is one of the most common responses a prospect will offer. Prospects aren't dumb; they know that a stall is an easy, nonargumentative way to blow-off an uneducated salesperson. In fact, they're right; most amateur salespeople will buy-in to this clever blow-off and go away with a smile on their faces. Inexperienced salespeople meekly accept this response thinking it's a good thing—they chomp down on the bait. Because they didn't hear "No," it's a positive response to them, a small victory. But it's not a victory; it's a trap. The neophyte salesperson gets swept up and usually defaults into one of two common response types: consenter or challenger.

CONSENTERS

They fold up their tents and pull out their calendars, asking, "So, when should I call you back, Bob?" Well, guess what, Bob doesn't care when you call him back because, in his mind, he's successfully blown you off and he probably won't take your call when you do follow-up.

If your prospect does accept your call—weeks later—any emotion that would've helped cement a decision is long gone. He might not even remember what the conversation was about or why it would benefit him to move forward with you. In many cases, you would have to start all over again, and the busy prospect doesn't have time for you.

CHALLENGERS

These alpha dogs have an entirely different approach than consenters—in fact, the exact opposite. Challengers want to jump on the stall and debate it. They ask, "What is it that you want to think about, Bob? Is it my company, my products?" Arguing the stall, asking those kinds of questions, will surely come across as combative to the prospect.

If you take this approach, your prospect will feel backed into a corner. It's important to note that he said, "I want to think it over" because it's something he's been programmed to say. Bob doesn't intend to "think" anything over after you leave. His stall was simply a motor response that relieves him of the burden of making a decision on the spot.

Neither of these faulty approaches will be fruitful. The first one, the docile one, will leave you with a boatload of *maybes* floating around in your Pipeline. (And eventually, an equal number of disappointments.) The second response, the argumentative one, might get you and your company disinvited from ever walking in the door again. Bottom line—neither of these tactics is professional or effective.

We suggest that you *ignore* the stall like it never happened. (*Almost;* I'm being facetious.) We *really* don't suggest you ignore the stall *completely*, but we certainly don't want you to take the bait, either. Instead, we will teach you to use the *ARC Method* to move your prospect gracefully and smoothly to a place where you can use a trial close and move your prospect back onto the main closing highway.

ARC is an acronym for Agree, Recall, and Connect. These are the three things you will automatically do, in this exact sequence, to set up an open-ended question, which is also a trial close. Below is an outline of the initial flow of the script:

- *Agree* and disarm
- *Recall* and remind
- *Connect* them to the WIIFM (What's In It For Me)

- Ask an *open-ended* question
- Close again

Let's take a moment to break down each of these steps so that you can develop a mental picture of how this works.

AGREE AND DISARM

This is where you relieve all the pressure that your prospect might feel. It's where your prospect thinks you're totally taking the bait. But, it's actually the reverse. You're baiting the hook for your prospect. It sounds like this:

> You: "That's perfectly understandable. Please take all of the time you need to think about this. It's important for you/your organization/your family..."

RECALL AND REMIND

This is where you recall and remind your prospect of one or more of the expressed needs or opportunities. (Arrows) These are needs or opportunities that you uncovered during your fact-finding discovery and engagement. You are going to ask your prospect to agree that there is a viable solution or opportunity on the table. This is what it might sound like:

> **You:** "You mentioned earlier that your company was having some challenge with _____." Or, "You mentioned there's an opportunity to improve your situation regarding _____. Did I understand that correctly?"

CONNECT THEM TO THE WIIFM

After you have recalled your prospect's needs or the opportunities, you are then ready to connect that to a tangible benefit that will solve that specific problem or fill the need. By doing that, you answer the, "What's in it for me?" question (WIIFM). It sounds like this:

> **You:** "With the unique (product-service-solutions) we've discussed, we can take care of your challenge and/or improve the company's position regarding _____."

With these three, unpretentious ARC statements; you've begun to gently guide your prospect back to the main highway. Remember, you want your prospect to either say "Yes" or tell you what the real challenge is (i.e., the specific objection). You're now back in control and headed in the right direction. Connecting them to the WIIFM is powerful, but your work isn't done yet. You have one last important task.

THE OPEN-ENDED QUESTION (Trial Close)

This is the payoff for this method. You will ask a well-phrased, open-ended question, a question that they can't give a one-word answer to. Control of the closing process is vitally important. You can maintain control in the midst of a stall (in almost any scenario) by asking open-ended questions. This is what it should sound like:

> **You:** "How do you see this solution being of benefit to you/your organization/your family?" (Ask this, and then sit back and shut up!)

The next response will almost always be positive or honest. Your prospects will either agree to move forward or, as if by magic, they'll tell you what their real objections are. (A good thing) Think about it. Almost any other response would be illogical. They've already said, "I want to think about it," so they can't use that nugget again. They're compelled to respond with their concerns or say, "Yes." If they concur that you've suggested a viable solution that's beneficial for them, then close them again.

When your prospect gives you the real objection, then you can go to that column of the CAP Closing Matrix© and follow the steps—clarify, isolate, use the proper rebuttal, and so on. Either a "Yes" or a real objection is far better than "I want to think it over." One of these two results will occur over 85–90 percent of the time when the ARC Method is used correctly.

The ARC Method is an effective closing tool that will help you overcome stalls and other nonspecific responses. You'll have the ability to regain control and move past *"I want to think about it"* without becoming combative. You can steer your prospects back onto the main highway and ask them to buy again. Remember, you simply have to have more ways of asking them to buy than they have of saying "No."

I have found that the real difference between a pro's closing strategy and an amateur's is the pro actually *has* a strategy. Each time a professional asks for the sale, the pro is stripping away the prospect's armor and soothing concerns. They're also cementing the worth and significance of their product or program. I love what Zig Ziglar has to say about this specific point:

> **"Each close you use should be an educational process by which**
> **you are able to raise the value in the prospect's mind."**

The CAP Closing Matrix© creates a flawless *sequence* that can be applied to any response to generate a positive result. Don't forget to visit our website and download a PDF of this matrix at:

> *www.thecapequation.com/resources/*

The reason it is so critical to drive to a definite result is that a new salesperson can easily be pacified into thinking that a "maybe" is a victory; however, if that's the mind-set, then the salesperson is on a muddy dirt road with no map and no gas. The 20 percent would rather get a "No" and learn a little about their prospect's objections. The pros know that a "No" is, at the very least, a definite metric result that gets them closer to a "Yes" based on their closing ratio. A professional closer knows that a practiced rebuttal can be used to overcome common objections. Then, a professional closer simply asks the prospect to buy again and stays on the main highway.

There is one other very important element that all pros use—we alluded to it earlier. We told you that prospects buy based on emotion and then justify their decision using logic and good business reasons. For this reason, your presentations, your questions, and your rebuttals should all be delivered with an element of emotion.

Maybe some of the points in this chapter sound like things you believe you should be taught to do by the organization you're part of. (Any logical person would assume this.) Nevertheless, let me assure you that over 90 percent of all new salespeople that hit the street can't regurgitate the five basic buying decisions their prospect has to make. They also couldn't dissect their presentations into its individual elements and they don't have at least three ways to ask for the sale. What's worse, most aren't even close to understanding what the closing process and sequence should look like, and they have not committed their rebuttals to memory and personalized them.

If you're simply cognizant of these vital areas of competency within your first 30–90 days of selling, you'll be light years ahead of your peers. You won't miss easy closing opportunities because you were unprepared to overcome basic objections. You will also start closing some of the tougher ones because you have a process and a sequence to default to.

Okay, you are on the road to being a good closer. Let's next discuss some things that have to be done after the commission is safely in your pocket. We will cover some Competencies that will truly set you apart from the rest.

CAP CLOSING MATRIX©

There are only **4 POSSIBLE** Responses...

YES	NO	CONDITION	STALL
Hit the **EASY** button, SHUT-UP and complete the paperwork	Clarify	Clarify	**Use ARC**
	Ask **more questions**	Ask **more questions**	Agree & Disarm
	Isolate	Isolate	Recall & Remind
	Use Appropriate **Rebuttal**	Set NEW **Commitment Objective**	Connect Them with WIIFM
	Close again	Set **NEXT** Appointment	Ask **Open-ended** Question
	Repeat process with **ALL** Objections		Close again
		Get summary **Commitment** from prospect	If **Stall** occurs again, repeat **ARC**
			Close again
	Close again		If they give you a **Specific Objection** go to **2nd** Column and follow that path and **Close** again
			If they offer a **Condition** go to **3rd** Column and follow that path **Close** again

For more resources, go to: → www.CAPequation.com

CHAPTER 12

The Cement

Sales Fulfillment and Service

*"How much do you, as a consumer, value a positive experience
with a brand or its customer service department? How
willing are you to share that with your friends?"*

—**SIMON MAINWARING,** branding consultant, social media expert

This chapter is dedicated to taking care of business after the sale is consummated. I like to call this "cementing the relationship." This is where you get to over deliver and stand out from the 80 percent.

The Competencies addressed here are just as important as all the rest; in fact, they might even be more important if you are involved in a business that requires some degree of fulfillment or enrollment after the initial sale. If your ultimate commission check is dependent on some installation of your product or service, you will need to develop just as much game here as anywhere else in the Competency arena.

These Competencies don't only apply to the needs of a B2B salesperson. If you sell to individuals or are involved in network marketing, there's usually a great opportunity to reinforce your relationship and gain great influence with your target client or associate by over delivering in fulfillment and service. In my opinion, service after the sale is becoming a lost art; hence, being excellent at this will further separate you from the pack. Great service also sets up the ability for you to ask for and receive referrals in volume.

These three Competencies work hand-in-hand with each other to establish your professional platform, a reputation that can carry you to riches. Let's dig in.

SALES FULFILLMENT

Whether you're selling products and services to business owners, individuals, or you're building a multilevel marketing (MLM) organization, there's usually some level of after sale responsibility. While it's difficult for me to become too specific based on the varied number of industries that comprises the audience of this book, I want to conceptualize why this Competency is so important. Once you understand the significance of fulfillment, you'll want to seek out the proper resources and practice the proper protocols.

I've certainly seen my share of hit-and-run artists in my tenure as a sales leader, and it has never made sense to me. Think about it—why would someone go all the way down the road of prospecting, presenting, and closing a prospect, getting the fish on the hook, and then simply not bother getting the fish into the boat? I chalk it up to wiring; however, regardless of the reasons, this is a poor habit. You cannot sustain yourself in most sales positions if you don't fulfill or install the product you sold.

In the way of an example, I will tell you about a salesperson who we worked with in the employee benefits industry for many years. We'll call him "Nolan." He was only an average presenter and closer, but what he lacked in high-level closing skills, he made up for in his prospecting volume and tenacity. He opened many key accounts for us simply because he out prospected a lot of people.

His challenges always began after the sale when he had to focus on establishing fulfillment conditions and educate staff. It was as if his brain clicked off once the initial employer contract was signed. As a result, his enrollments were sloppy and less productive than they could have been, leading the employer to wonder if the time offered to educate employees was productive or even worth it. The ongoing service after the sale was yet another big challenge. Nolan's clients perceived that he fumbled the football after they said "Yes." They liked him personally, but because of his poor follow-up after the sale, they perceived him as incompetent, which resulted in their asking for a new rep. This cycle was painful for all involved.

Nolan could have had a much better career. Simply based on his tenacity and prospecting disciplines, he could have made a ton of money. Think about it—he was willing to do the hard stuff (prospecting and setting appointments) that most others aren't. Nolan is still around, but his managers have to follow close behind him and clean up his messes. They have to pair him with someone who can do the after-sale fulfillment. He has to split all of his earnings with that person. His lack of competence costs him half of all his commissions! In addition—as you can well imagine—he doesn't generate a lot of referrals, so he's still making massive cold calls even after fifteen years in the industry.

The significance of this cautionary tale is that if your sales process requires any sort of fulfillment after the sale, then you must become practiced at it. If you choose not to, you either won't make it in sales, or you won't be able to scale your business or generate the kind of good reputation that yields referrals.

DELIVERING SERVICE

I believe the problem with the word "service" is that most salespeople frame this word as a negative one in their own minds. For example, I've heard this expressed in the following way: "Oh, shoot. I have to drive out to ABC Company today and get a signature on a form and meet with one new employee. What a big, gigantic waste of my precious time. Ugh."

Look, regardless of what you are selling and whom you are selling those things to, any opportunity to serve clients should be looked at as not a chore, burden, or imposition on your time, but as an honor, or even better, an opportunity. Here are the three main reasons you should consider offering unparalleled service to your clients or business associates:

1. First and foremost, offering great service is the *right thing to do!* You've been paid a commission for the sale. Your advance compensation and trailing commissions take into consideration that you *will* deliver service to that client. Your client also deserves the best service you can offer. That's why they chose you as a vendor in the first place. If you withhold your best level of service, you are cheating your client and also cheating the organization you work for.

2. You only have one *reputation* to develop and be known by in your marketplace. If you offer your clients or associates poor service or inadequate follow-up, your reputation will suffer. *When your reputation becomes tarnished, it's almost impossible to repair it.* Remember, good news travels fast, but bad news travels even faster. When you offer excellent service, you are setting yourself apart from the majority of vendors or suppliers that your client works with.

3. Top sales professionals, the 20 percent, don't view a service call as merely a service call; they see it as an additional sales opportunity. *Pros use service calls to further solidify their relationships with their clients.* They see it as a perfect opportunity to offer timely responses and ask for *more referrals.* Pros work *warm* as often as they can and they get lots of referrals. Conversely, if you didn't do a great job at the fulfillment of the sale, and if you didn't follow up with them cheerfully and in a timely manner, why the heck would they give you any?

If #3 doesn't click for you or make you think, then please close this book and hand it to someone who actually wants to get wealthy in sales.

CHAPTER 13

Getting Warmer

Referrals on Demand

"Internalize the Golden Rule of sales that says: All things being equal, people will do business with, and refer business to, those people they know, like and trust."

—**BOB BURG,** speaker and author, Endless Referrals

Referrals are like gold. They are like precious gems that are sitting right in front of you, there for the taking. But the sad truth is that most salespeople do not bend over and pick them up. Let's first walk through some of the basics of generating referrals—the most important factors—and then we can go a few layers deeper. Here are the five rudimentary guidelines of referral marketing.

1. Referrals Must Be a Priority for You

You must think of building your referral business as a vital factor to your success. This must be your philosophy versus considering referrals nothing more than an ancillary lead source in addition to cold calling. Referral marketing and selling should become your primary mode of business development versus a secondary one.

2. A System Has to Be in Place

A well-developed referral system must be set in place. If you have no measured strategy to gain referrals in volume, and your plan is simply to ask for referrals in a haphazard manner, then you might ask for them in the wrong way. This can result in a blown opportunity and a permanently closed door.

3. Referrals Are a Daily Program

Building your business through referral selling should be an integral part of your everyday operations, not just a campaign that takes place once in a while when you feel like it. It needs to become as much of a habit as brushing your teeth.

4. Skill Development Is Necessary

Obtaining referrals is not easy. The relationships that your contacts have are very personal to them. They aren't going to simply hand them over to you just because you ask. You need to forge a deeper connection with the person you are asking, and that takes some work. You will also have to develop a skill set around the way you ask. You should work toward skill betterment in this area just as you do in all other areas.

5. Overcome the Fear of Asking

In addition to being afraid of objections during a presentation, new salespeople might not be comfortable asking for referrals because they assume they'll get turned down or that their client is too busy. In my experience, people are actually very happy to help provide introductions if they can because it's one way they can help others in an increasingly impersonal environment.

Think about all the steps in the sales process that are cut out when you don't have to walk into a sale "cold": You don't have to get past a gatekeeper. You usually don't have to wait months to gain access. You don't have to convince the decision maker that you are trustworthy. You don't have to sell them on the fact that your programs are needed and wanted.

In addition, your closing ratio will double on your warm approaches.

Bottom line—referrals are *gold*, but for your client or contact to willfully introduce you to others they know, you have to be willing to *ask* for the referral and you must ask for it in the right way. I've suggested that you need to develop a system, and there are some great books out there for help with this. The books we endorse are on our recommended book list. Please go to our resource link below for the full list:

www.thecapequation.com/resources/

A few of the books we suggest will assist you in creating an advanced referral selling system as you move past your first six months in your sales career. For now, let's focus on the five-step process we teach and focus on two things, *when* to ask for referrals and *how* to ask for them.

When to Ask

There is a right and wrong time to ask for referrals. Obviously, if you are with a client to fix a problem or challenge or to field a complaint, this is definitely the *wrong* time to ask. Conversely, when you have successfully completed the fulfillment of the sale and are visiting with your client, this is an ideal time to use your referral system.

How to Ask

I mentioned earlier in this section that you must ask for referrals in the *right* way. The following sample dialogue will demonstrate the manner in which most salespeople, (the 80%) ask for referrals:

Salesperson: "Whom do you know who you think might be interested in my products or services?"

Prospect: "Well, let me think about *that and get back to you.*"

Salesperson: "Sure...sounds good. Here are a few of my business cards. Could you pass them along to anyone you think *is interested?*"

And there you have it...a complete exercise in futility. There is no plan, no cohesive strategy, and no definite call to action.

The reason this way to ask rarely works is that you've asked your prospect to focus on too *wide* a target—everyone in the world whom they know. Think about it—if I ask you whom you know who "might be interested," I'm asking you to sort through a mental Rolodex of hundreds of people you might know. Busy people don't function that way. Their attention filters block out your question; their protective mechanisms kick in and register that there isn't enough time to sort through such a vast array of contacts. So, they shut down and say something like, "Hey, yeah, let me think about it and get back to you. Give me a few of your cards." They would actually like to help you; you simply haven't made it easy enough for them to do so.

Let's solve that challenge with a simple five-step program that you can initiate your very first month in sales. This recommended process is simple and straightforward, but it is comprised of all the advanced elements that more sophisticated systems contain. It can be adapted to any product, market, or form of distribution and can be built and implemented in a matter of days.

THE FIVE-STEP REFERRAL PROCESS

1. Develop Referral-Letter Templates

The template on the following page can serve as a quick and easy way for your clients to endorse your services when they refer you. Make sure that there exists some degree of loyalty to your products and services. Asking for referrals in this way also reinforces their commitment to your company or organization.

Referral Letter Template:

To (Future Client):

When I was first approached by (your name), I was not interested in purchasing _____ or partnering with _____. I/We did not feel that we needed or wanted to participate in _____, especially at their cost. Through professional persistence, I chose to meet with (your name). After meeting with (your name) I was impressed with their products and services.

To my surprise, I have been very satisfied with the level of service _____ has provided me, personally, and the service they've provided my company. From start to finish, implementing _____ had a positive impact on our (organization/family) and it was easy to get started/use/install.

I would highly recommend that you look at adding _____ for the well being of your (family/employees/business). If you have any questions on how _____ can benefit you as an (individual/business owner) please don't hesitate to contact me personally.

Sincerely,

Individual/Business Owner's Name
Title, Company Name

Of course, you will need to tweak this letter and customize it to the products, services, and market you are serving, but I think you can get a sense of what it will look like.

2. Complete a Wish List

Compile a list of twelve to fifteen names of individuals, companies, or target organizations that are in their center of influence that you'd like to meet. Here are the sources to use in order of their effectiveness:

- List of individuals or business owners from your contact's connections on *LinkedIn*
- List of individuals or companies in *close proximity* (geographically) to the account
- List of individuals or companies within the *same industry* or circle as the contact you are meeting with

3. Precall Prep and Set-up

Print out Referral Letters and Wish List.

4. *The Ask*

Ask your client to help you.

> **YOU:** "Well (your contact), now that you understand that there is a real need for our (products/services) and that the (products/services) are first class, perhaps you can help me out. Before our meeting today, I e-mailed you some information to review. Did you get a chance to look through it?"
>
> **THEM:** "Yes, I did."
>
> **YOU:** "Great. I've learned that by fostering new business through a referral base, I've developed more time to provide my clients with excellent service. Would you be able to introduce me to others you have a strong relationship with?"
>
> **THEM:** "I don't know of anyone off the top of my head."
>
> **YOU:** "No problem. In that case, let me show you my target-client list. I know these potential clients fit the profile of whom could use our programs, but I need help getting in front of them. Do you know anyone on this list you could introduce me to?"
>
> **THEM:** "Bob's on this list, and he's a good fiend of mine. I'm sure I could get him to meet with you."
>
> **YOU:** "Great. I would just need your assistant to print out the reference letter on your letterhead to sign, and we're all set."

The *Ask* is as simple and straightforward as that. The reason this type of ask works and the *wrong* way doesn't work is that you have not asked the busy person to think of *everyone* in the world whom they know. You have bypassed their attentional filters that kick in and protect them from time-consuming tasks, and you've made their jobs very easy. You've focused them on a very small and *select* list of people who are qualified to hear about your product or service.

You aren't even asking them to make a call or to draft a letter. You've taken the work off their desks by simply asking them to print out the pre-written letter on their letterhead and sign it.

*A few additional notes...*when everything goes according to your plan:

- Always carry a blue ink pen for the business owner to sign the letters with. It looks more authentic and less like a photocopy.
- If the business owner knows three people on your checklist and agrees to introduce you to those owners, get four letters— one letter for each Introduction and an extra to add to your referral- letter book.
- Get a company envelope to put the letters in if possible.
- *Always* send a thank-you card for their help.

*A few additional notes...*when things *don't* go according to plan:

- If they haven't read the letter by the time you show up, then simply use your hard copy to show the business owner and get approval. If they don't know anyone on your list (which is unlikely, since you'll use a combination of accounts nearby and other accounts in the area), but, if it happens, remember to ask specifically whom they know. For example: (from A to Z) "Who is your *a*ttorney?" "Who is your *b*anker?" "Who is your *c*ar dealer?" "Who is your *d*entist?"
- If they don't have letterhead or company envelopes, you can make a letterhead or print it on blank paper. If they do not have envelopes, just use a blank one. If they are hesitant, then simply assure them that you would do nothing to make them look bad: (1) it could hurt the business you currently have with them, and (2) you risk never receiving another referral from them. Also, tell them how you'd approach the person they referred you to. For example, tell them you'd say the following:

"The other day, I was helping (their name) with _____ (your products/services). It worked out great for them. Since it was such a good fit, they thought you might want to take a quick ten minutes to find out how it works. Of course, _____ (your client's name) and I aren't assuming anything. We can just go over the programs and see if they are a fit."

Your clients might have had a bad experience with referring people in the past. Put their minds at ease and tell them how the process works.

5. *Approaching the Referral*

You've been successful getting the letters on letterhead, and now you need to start approaching the business owners you've been referred to. Remember the following:

- Put the letter in an envelope. (Some write "Confidential" on it.) This really intrigues the gatekeepers and business owners.
- Never give the letter to the gatekeeper. Simply show it to them.
- If the business owner is not in, just say, "I can come back," and walk out.

Here's a sample dialogue to use in a few different scenarios when you approach your referral:

When the business owner is not in...

YOU: "My name is _____ and I have a letter from Beverly Jones from _____ that she wanted me to hand deliver to Bob Simpson." (Hold up the letter.)

GATEKEEPER: "Bob is not in. I can give it to him."

YOU: "They asked that I hand deliver it. I can come back. When is a better time?"

When the business owner is in...

YOU: "Hello, Bob, My name is _____. Beverly Jones from _____ gave me a letter that she wanted me to hand deliver to you." (Hand them the letter and wait for them to read it. Most likely, they'll crack a little smile, knowing that one of their friends has sent a salesperson over to harass them.)

REFERRAL: "So, I guess you know Beverly or do business with her. She's in my BNI group."

YOU: "Great. Well, obviously Beverly really benefitted from our services and thought it would help if we talked. Of course, I'm assuming nothing, and these programs are at no cost to you. I'd like to get fifteen minutes on your calendar, or I'm ready now if you have time.

REFERRAL: "Actually, I have time now."

YOU: "Great. Can we use your office?"

This is a very simple, five-step referral system. You can begin using this system with the very first sale you close, and you should! Because, after all, you don't want to cold-call for the rest of your life, do you?

We're almost ready to move past Competencies and on to Attitudes. The good news is that all you have to do is become *adequate* in the areas we've covered. You don't have to become an expert. We can help you become an authority in year two, but let's get you there first! So, congratulations! You are one-third of the way to ensuring yourself a sustained career in commission sales. You have shifted many odds into your favor.

In Part II of this book we have identified and explored what we believe are the most critical competencies, the elements of the physical game that you will need to become adequately proficient at. While Competencies are the first component of The CAP Equation©, we must add another component to the mix of things. We are going to go inside now and discuss Attitudes, the mental side of this game.

PART III

Attitudes - C + A × P

CHAPTER 14

A Product of...

Where Attitudes Start

*"It's better to hang out with people better than you.
Pick out associates whose behaviors are better than
yours and you'll drift in that direction."*

—**WARREN BUFFETT,** investor and philanthropist

I want to take you back to my summer of 1979. It was a time when I was transitioning from standing on the car lot waiting for a prospect to walk on to a guy carrying a briefcase full of insurance applications while knocking on doors. My entrance into the insurance and financial product industry wasn't well planned. I answered a blind ad in the newspaper and wound up being hired by a gentleman named, Bud Cole.

Bud was the agency director at the small Accident Policy Division of

Pennsylvania Life. Two weeks after he hired me he directed me to go purchase the very book pictured below. And I did.

For reference, the year I purchased this book, girls were wearing leg warmers, Jimmy Carter was president, and we were still cleaning up the mess in Vietnam. There was no cable, streaming, or DVR. Arnold Palmer was still playing golf on the PGA Tour, a "cell" phone was what you used to make calls from jail and digital computing meant counting on your fingers. There was no e-mail, Twitter, Facebook, Vine, Instagram, Pinterest, Tumblr, or LinkedIn. It was the dark ages of information. In 1979, if you wanted to learn something, you had to get a book, and then you had to open up the book and read it.

The paperback pictured is dog-eared—completely worn out. Most of the pages are falling out. I've had the book in my possession for thirty-five years. I've been reading it—turning its pages—for that long. It's stored on my bookshelf in a plastic bag. Did you happen to notice the price of the book in the upper-left-hand corner? If it's too small to read, it says $3.00. I think I might have gotten my money's worth out of the book, but I'll come back to that in a moment.

I had never read a self-help book before the summer of '79. Nobody had ever suggested I do so, but Bud Cole did, and for that I am eternally grateful. This first book, *Think and Grow Rich*, turned me on to a world where anything I could imagine doing was possible. It began my journey in the understanding of how successful people think and act.

After I devoured Napoleon Hill's seminal work and a few of his others, I moved on to read authors such as Og Mandino, W. Clement Stone, and Zig Ziglar. As years went on, I bought books, tapes, and CDs produced by speakers and authors like Tony Robbins, Denis Waitley, Ken Blanchard, John Maxwell, Wayne Dyer, Brian Tracy, and Stephen Covey. I became a voracious reader and an eager student of the mind. I studied the thought processes and belief systems that separated top salespeople and leaders (Pareto's 20 percent) from all of the rest.

I had originally and mistakenly assumed that the estrangement of top producers from the rest of the pack occurred because they outworked the rest. After digging into my first few books, I soon learned that it went far beyond that. Much more of top performers' success could be attributed to how they managed their thoughts, feelings, and responses. In short, their success was all about the *attitudes* they settled on and the behavioral habits they developed and practiced.

I began to understand that top performers simply behaved differently from the rest. Reading these first books helped me identify what cerebral fundamentals top producers and great thinkers practiced and what elements made up their games.

In this section of the book, we explore the second component of The CAP Equation©. I'm going to help you understand why the *mental* aspects of the sales game are so critical to your survival. I outline why the 20 percent vigilantly select the belief systems they settled on.

The mental game is abstract, much harder to grasp than the hard-wired Competencies you've been asked to learn. A new salesperson is going to naturally focus on absorbing and learning things like product knowledge, presentation skills, and closing methods. This practice of becoming solid in your core Competencies (as we explored in previous chapters) is certainly important, but it's only one-third of the equation. It is my belief that it's just as critical—if not more so—to learn how to think, feel, and respond to all the uncontrollable factors that will frame your career.

The proper, overall thought process begins with the confidence level you have in your Competencies. It continues with the level of passion you have for the industry and your company, then it hinges on the degree of focus you have day in and day out. The most imperative thought process has to do with your emotional controls, your ability to reframe experiences on the fly so that you can maintain an even emotional flow, never allowing yourself to get too low or too high. All of these thought processes and beliefs come together to form your overall attitude about commission sales.

Before we go too much further down the line discussing attitudes, let's look at the definition of this key word:

at·ti·tude

A settled way of thinking or feeling about something,
typically one that is reflected in a person's behavior

—MERRIAM WEBSTER'S DICTIONARY

What the *Webster's* definition tells us is that the collection of our thoughts and feelings will construct a settled or *complete* way of thinking. This will form a mind-set that will reveal itself in our behavior and actions. In plainer words, what we allow ourselves to think and feel will completely shape the way we speak and act, and there is no way around it.

However, there's more that happens after that. As our behavior plays out, it reinforces the validity of our thoughts and feelings. Our actions lend *credence* to our thoughts and feelings, whatever they might be. What you think and feel (positive or negative) makes you speak and behave a certain way, and then those actions create momentum to support your original belief. It's awesome if your belief systems are ones that support your desired goals and objectives; however, it is devastating if those attitudes and behaviors are destructive ones. It won't matter how competent, skillful, or knowledgeable you are, if your attitudes are faulty, you'll crash and burn anyway.

Elite salespeople, the 20 percent, know how to think, feel, and respond. They've reconciled on a way of thinking and feeling about their profession that supports their objectives. They have developed an overall attitude about sales, and this plays out in their everyday behavior.

Put in athletic terms: the *mental* or *inner* game is every thought process that competitors allow into their brains just before and during their competitions. Their carefully chosen thoughts trigger feelings, which produce physical responses. Top competitors in all sports have already vigilantly settled on the thoughts, feelings, and behaviors they will manifest during a game.

A top NBA player has predetermined that if his team scores on their possession they'll stalk the inbound passer and keep backcourt pressure on their offensive assignment. An elite, major league baseball player who has just struck out will stride back to his dugout with head held high. He is replaying each pitch type, noting speed and location, knowing that strikeouts are part of the game—confident that he'll get another chance to swing the bat in a few innings.

A great example of an athlete who understands the power of mastering the *inner* game is Derek Jeter. While his physical gifts are evident, what you can't see is even more impressive. He arrived in the nation's largest media market at the age of 20 and put in 20 seasons there. The New York Yankee baseball great remained under a microscope for his entire career. No other ballplayer spent more time in the public eye than Jeter. He was also the most influential and popular player in his sport's greatest era of growth.

All athletes suffer slumps. Nobody, even those who make their sport's Hall of Fame, as surely Jeter will, are immune to these temporary collapses in performance. Just imagine being the most visible player in your sport in the biggest media market when a mild slump occurred. It would be easy to become negative and shut down. You and I could easily become sealed off to our boss, our teammates or anyone else from the outside. But, Jeter never did that. He rarely if ever became negative, even in the slightest way. Here's what Derek Jeter had to say to the press during one interview when the media was asking about his confident demeanor during a streak of poor performance:

> "When people are negative a lot it starts to creep into their mind and then they start having doubts, and I don't like that. If there's another way, show me. My job is to stay positive. My job is to limit distractions. And if you get annoyed by that, I don't expect you to understand because you're not in my shoes."

Derek Jeter totally got it.

He knew that his ability to hit a baseball was solid. He didn't suddenly forget how to do it. He knew that if he stayed positive and continued to work hard at batting practice each day, his numbers would turn around. He wasn't going to begin thinking, acting or speaking negatively and he wasn't going to allow someone else to bait him into it.

All professional athletes and entertainers have to perform day in and day out during their time on stage, just as a professional salesperson has to do. It would be easy for them to become a product of their environment, but they choose not to. They choose to carefully create and control their environment.

Let's first examine two key practices you can engage in that will lay the foundation for the formation of your environment. These are the two most influential factors that can form your processes. They are, the books you read, (and other input) and the people you associate with.

1. The Books You Read (And the Input You Allow In)

Let me jump back to the book pictured on the first page of this chapter, *Think and Grow Rich*, the one Bud Cole directed me to purchase. It fired up my imagination; It gave me a glimpse of what I could do, what I could become; it caused me to want to read another book, and then another, and another. I haven't stopped reading and self-educating since that summer of '79. Here's my strong suggestion to you: read from a carefully selected list of books for at least fifteen minutes when you wake up in the morning and at least fifteen minutes before you go to bed each night.

I quickly built a library of books that I believed would support the kind of thinking and philosophies I would need to develop to survive and thrive in commission sales. I read books authored by those who had earned millions in sales and sales leadership. I attempted to climb into their heads. I strived to begin thinking, feeling, and responding like they did—modeling them—so that I could replicate their results.

Of course, back in 1979, books had to be bought at the good old bookstore or ordered through the mail. Cutting-edge information on sales and leadership concepts were harder to access, and relatively speaking, more expensive. Because of the many forms of consumable digital media that are available today, and also because of the exponential nature of the Internet, we now have thousands of sites that cater to almost any specific topic or general subject you'd like to study. In addition, there is a lot of free information available through industry publications, articles and blogs.

While expanding access to information is helpful, it can also be a two-edged sword. There's simply too much information (TMI) out there, and some of it is not credible. In addition, some of this TMI comes at your ears and eyes even if you don't want it to. I'm referring to spam, unsolicited e-mail from friends and associates, and the flow of information and news that emanates from television, radio, Twitter, Facebook, and so on. While you have to be careful to seek out and choose the right books to read, you have to be just as aware of the onslaught of digital information that will unavoidably fly into your face.

There is also the challenge of staying energetic and positive. The infinite number of news media outlets that barrage us constantly doesn't make this task easy. We are inundated by bad news and worse news. This type of mental input is unhealthy and distracting. It drains us of energy without us even knowing it. In this digital age, we need to become keenly aware of not only what we are reading, but also what input we are allowing to *enter* our minds. I believe I'd be completely lost if I weren't feeding my head with inspirational stories and new creative ideas each day.

I have referenced our recommended reading list on several occasions throughout this text. If you have not yet gone to our website and viewed the selected book list, I recommend that you do it now.

www.thecapequation.com/resources/

2. THE PEOPLE YOU ASSOCIATE WITH AND MODEL

It's obvious that the best of the best need and want coaching as well as input from other top performers. This is illustrated by the fact that elite athletes seek out people to help them become better. Shouldn't you be doing the same? It might be obvious to you that you need to build a great coaching relationship with your direct manager as well as the managers a level or two above you, but you would also be wise to ask top producers for a few minutes of their time.

Please know that elite performers are somewhat selective, even stingy, about whom they spend their time with, so you must demonstrate to them you are serious before asking them for their time. You will also notice that top salespeople are harder to find. They don't hang out in the office just to hang out. There is no wasted motion in their day.

Along with developing some alliances with top producers at work, you should begin to develop something we call your *Personal Board of Directors*. This is a very select group of men or women whom you have a great deal of respect for. I urge you to start identifying people who are mature and stable in business as well as life. These are people who would be happy to offer you a listening ear and counsel when asked.

These select people can help you ask yourself the right questions when you have a career challenge or a life issue you need to solve or get past. These select mentors are usually outside the company or organization you work for, but can also be part of your business. Having mentors outside your organization will be even more important as you move into year two and beyond. You will need eyes and ears that are completely unattached to what you do, unbiased in their thoughts and opinions.

I will digress one last time and refer to the book pictured on the first page of this chapter.

One day, Bud Cole walked over to where I was standing, which was always right next to the donuts. Bud was six foot nine; I'm five foot seven on a good day. He stood there, inches away, towering over me, glaring at me. He motioned me away from the donuts that Monday morning without saying anything. When we were out in the hallway, he asked me if I'd read the book he told me to buy, *Think and Grow Rich*. I told him I had. He interrogated me—gave me a pop quiz—to see if I were lying. He wanted to know what I took away from the book. When he was satisfied with my rather long-winded answers, he smiled.

Bud wore a pair of granny glasses for reading. They hung on a chain around his neck. He had this habit of folding the glasses up and using them as a poker, jabbing you in the chest when he wanted to make a point. He leaned in, real close to me. He folded up those damn glasses and started poking me in the chest. He whispered to me like he was passing on a CIA secret. He said:

"In five years from now you'll be a product of the books you read and the people you associate with. So choose both of them carefully."

It was only 8:35 a.m., and I only had one cup of coffee and a jelly donut down the hatch. There were still a few choice pastries left in the meeting room, and I wanted to hurry back in there. I nodded my head to placate him, not completely digesting his cautionary counsel. Actually, I was just hoping he'd stop poking me in the chest with the sharp end of his granny glasses.

His advice marinated in my brain for a few months until I was able to determine how I could apply it. Bud's little gem that morning in 1979 eventually became a huge part of my core belief system. Bud had handed me the combination to the safe. He was plainly telling me to make a conscious decision to read the books that would prepare my mind to accept the success that would follow. He was telling me to study and model the best salespeople. He was telling me what I'd become *a product of.*

With my newfound love of reading, and Bud's practices firmly ensconced in my brain, I was soon able to assemble a list of concepts, philosophies, and thought processes that would become instrumental to my breaking through. I did this by reading every day and selecting the people I wanted to associate with and model.

Over the years, I've read over one thousand books on subjects relating to sales, leadership, success, entrepreneurialism, and investing. That first book, *Think and Grow Rich*, was the catalyst. It was the foundation that ushered in an entirely different set of thoughts and outlooks for my life. The unassuming, worn-out paperback was the key element that enabled me to earn millions upon millions in sales commissions and overrides. The book cost me $3.00. I think I got my money's worth.

In the next few chapters, we identify and expand upon the belief systems that will make it possible for you to survive and thrive in commission sales. These next few chapters might be the most beneficial sales-related content you'll ever read. These will be the *million-dollar mind-sets* that transform your career if you allow them to.

CHAPTER 15

Think, Feel and Respond

How Attitudes Are Formed

"A man is but the product of his thoughts.
What he thinks, he becomes."

—**MAHATMA GANDHI,** civil rights leader

After I cracked that first book, I began voraciously reading. I started to grow personally as well as professionally. My newly adopted thought processes allowed me to feel and respond differently about the things that happened to and around me. My responses became less groundless and emotional. My reactions slowly became more logical and well-thought-out responses, ones that were more conducive to my stated objectives. My behavioral patterns gradually changed. I was able to do this because I chose to establish a set of attitudes that were modeled after top salespeople, sales leaders, and entrepreneurs. I had begun to think and grow rich. I'd begun to adopt million-dollar mind-sets.

Of course, none of this happened over night. The transformation took months and some of the trickier thought processes took years to master. No major transformation happens immediately, but from the juncture of reading that first book, the change had begun, and the makeovers have never stopped.

Since the day I purchased that first book, I've spent the rest of my sales career being the dumbest guy in the room. After Bud Cole showed me the light, I became a perpetual student. I shut my mouth, took notice of the stark lessons happening around me. Since that summer of 1979, I haven't stopped learning and seeking out personal mentors. I'm not going to lie to you. There have been times in my life I was more conscious, more receptive than others, but for the most part, I've been analyzing salespeople and leaders, learning what makes them tick, for thirty-five years. There isn't much about their thought processes, habits, and behaviors that have eluded my scrutiny or evaluation.

You've heard the phrase, "Success leaves clues," right? I don't agree with that axiom; it's not accurate. If you are at all aware of what's happening around you, then success leaves deep ruts in the road for you to follow. You have to be ignorant not to notice the big tire tracks in the road. The 20 percent are in tune with the industry. They know their products backward and forward. They're definitely better prospectors, presenters, and closers than the average. But those aren't even the most critical success factors for them. What truly separates the top producers from all of the rest is how they *think*, *feel*, and *respond* to circumstances around them; how they carry themselves; their attitudes and behavioral patterns.

If you are brand new to sales, and you simply decided to stalk a top producer and *model* the behaviors, you'd be light years ahead of all other entry-level salespeople. You'd be way ahead of the pack before you ever attended your first product-training class. Elite producers make a conscious decision to develop and refine their million-dollar mind-sets while the rest of the pack struggle with fifty-cent mentalities.

Sure, there is separation that will naturally occur in the area of Competencies. Great presenters and closers are inherently going to seize more opportunities than average closers. But then again, I've seen some fairly decent presenters and closers—very competent people—crash and burn while complaining about how psychologically challenging the game was. So, while becoming competent at your core skill sets is a critical factor, *the most dramatic split occurs over the span of only six inches—those six inches between your ears!*

Becoming adequate at the proficiencies listed in the previous chapters is more or less a *flat line* task. You can argue that some people might suffer from stage fright or call reluctance; however, for the most part, scripting can overcome those challenges. Learning your Competencies isn't an emotional or spiritual shift. It doesn't require change at a person's core level of beliefs. It isn't nearly as painful as changing your attitudes.

Consider this: if you have thought and felt a certain way about something your entire life, and then a mentor suggests that you think of that same thing in a totally different way, feel differently about it—well, that's painful!

Let's use failure and/or rejection as an example. We've experienced the word "No" and have been rejected since we could walk and talk. Our parents, teachers, coaches, and even spouses have used the word liberally with us over the years. It always signaled something negative to us, something we couldn't *have* or couldn't *do*. We're ingrained to feel bad when we hear the word "No", when we are rejected; we classically begin to respond with behavior that's less than positive; we begin to repel or move away from the person who's rejecting us or the thing we're failing at. We inherently lose confidence in our abilities.

Societal conditioning, especially with Millennials, hasn't made dealing with failure any easier for young people. The current brand of parenting tends to protect a child from anything that would resemble failure. I think this is referred to as "helicopter parenting" because mom and dad hover to make sure their kid doesn't fall down. There is no score kept in the tee ball game. Everybody is a winner; everyone gets a trophy after the soccer season is over.

But life doesn't work that way, and by the time we sign on the dotted line and become commission salespeople, we've been conditioned and co-cooned for many years, protected from the concept of failure and the nastiness of rejection. We look at failure and rejection as negative, something to shy away from at all costs.

So what are your sales trainer and manager going to ask you to do? They're going to ask you to view a "No", a rejection, as a neutral, even a positive outcome versus a failure. They are going to ask you to go get a lot of "Nos." They're going to ask you to think, feel, and respond in a way that is diametrically opposed to what you've grown to know and practice as a belief system.

Talk about painful. But this is the reality of it; this is just one type of many types of mind-sets you're going to be asked to change, shift, or transform. That's why Attitudes are the toughest part of The CAP Equation©. A hint: if you get the *A* down cold, the other two components (Competencies and Pipeline) will seem like child's play in comparison.

If I've convinced you that the trickiest and toughest part of The CAP Equation© is the *A*, and if you believe that if you master Attitudes the rest of the equation is a breeze, then you would logically deduce that there is no valid reason for there to be a separation between you and the top 20 percent. There is no immovable impediment between you and your financial aspirations. *The only barrier to your success will be your unwillingness to transform your thoughts, feelings, and responses.*

You will have to make a conscious decision to get out of your own way so that you can model the thought processes and attitudes that will enable you to survive and thrive in commission sales. If you can successfully break down any walls you've built up, then you are well on your way to the "promised land," the 20 percent.

In the second half of this chapter, I'm going to remove the other big roadblock that might exist. Earlier in this chapter, I mentioned that success leaves far more than clues—it leaves deep ruts in the road for us to follow. The tire tracks from success are all around you, if you are looking for them. Conversely, the skid marks of failure, pointing straight into the ditch, are there for you to see and take note of as well.

Those in the ditch have most likely not mastered their ways of thinking, feeling, and responding in ways that help them settle on the proper, overall attitudes. We will dedicate the balance of this chapter to how the 20 percent manage their thought processes. We will break down and explain how they keep themselves on the straight and narrow. We will expose and blueprint what they use to manage and apply the key attitudes that they all adopt and practice.

Before we get started, I must warn you, the thought processes you will learn from this book will sound very logical; they look simple and straightforward on paper. You'll convince yourself that they'll be easy to learn and follow. But they aren't easy to follow at all, and there's a reason for that.

When you read about, or somebody tells you about, a successful person's mental makeup, his or her mind-sets and attitudes, you're simply examining a reasonable concept that has worked for somebody else. You're studying it academically from a *safe* distance.

It's much like a rookie police officer being highly trained and instructed what to do when in an emergency situation; however, the training takes place at the police academy; it's a sterile environment. At the academy, there's time to drill and rehearse, even observe others practicing the disciplines. It is a whole different experience when it's real and a bad guy is pointing a gun at you. That's where the rookie must make definite choices. When it's game time, you must choose your thoughts, feelings, and responses carefully. The rookie police officer must have committed to a default thought process, and he or she must trust it completely.

As it applies to commission sales, let me pinpoint and expose the specific challenge of actually practicing a new thought process once you've decided to adopt it. The discussion that follows is a breakdown of the three parts—thoughts, feelings, and responses—using rejection as an example.

THOUGHTS

Thoughts come first in this process. You *adopt* the thought process of the 20 percent, which is that rejection is not a negative outcome to shrink away from. Rejection, prospects saying "No," is necessary and predict-able along the path to consistent metrics and your wins.

Sounds good on paper, right? We will go into this concept in depth next chapter, but you get the point. You will hear "No" more than you hear "Yes." The 20 percent don't react emotionally to rejection. They have a settled attitude about it. "Right on," you say..."I can do that." You prob-ably can until some other thoughts or feelings surface.

FEELINGS

This is where the process can take a very different path from your intend-ed route. You are a new or struggling salesperson and you hear "No" one too many times in a given week. Your emotional gas tank is a little low because of the fight you had with your spouse or your child misbehaved before you left for work that morning. The rejection you just received from a prospect creates some interesting thoughts in your head, and by "interesting," I mean negative.

In this example, those thoughts are opposed to the ones you commit-ted to adopt, the ones that looked good on paper. That foreign thought process then triggers a set of *feelings*. The feelings aren't positive; they are rather negative and destructive. They don't support the attitude you faith-fully promised to adopt and practice.

The destructive self-talk sounds something like this:

"Wow. Another 'No'! I haven't closed anything in three weeks, and my calendar and pipeline are near empty. What am I doing out here? My appointment-setting skills are slipping, and my presentation is all over the place. I'll never be a great salesperson. Star salespeople are born that way, and anyway, all the top people around here get fed all the juicy leads and catch all the breaks. I should just stop trying to make calls today. I'm just not very good at this."

This scenario illustrates that the salesperson has allowed the thoughts that popped into the mind (the ones in *conflict* with the beliefs the salesperson committed to practice) to trigger runaway negative feelings. Instead of taking a deep breath and stepping away for a moment to *inspect* and *replace* those destructive thoughts and feelings, those runaway feelings are allowed to take control and dictate a reaction.

RESPONSES

Of course, you can guess the rest. It's fairly obvious that our fictitious person has allowed the negative thoughts to trigger the byproduct, which are destructive feelings. The destructive feelings will then produce responses that are counterproductive to all of their stated goals.

> "I know it's only 1:30 in the afternoon, and I should try to set a few more appointments, but I just need to go home. This just isn't working for me today."

So, our fictitious salesperson with the empty emotional gas tank is going to pull up stakes and go home and drown his sorrows in a cold beer. This is the response he chooses, and this type of response, repeated, can be fatal to his career. A repeated response of this kind, shaped by negative thoughts and feelings, will form a destructive behavioral pattern. The repeated behavior eventually becomes an attitude (whether you like it or not). Good, bad, or indifferent, you will *own* the attitude; by default, you've adopted it.

The unhealthiest part of this mental exhibition is that once you begin repeatedly feeling and responding to something a certain way, your mind registers the behavior as perfectly *acceptable*; it's a Jedi mind trick. Your behavior actually *reinforces* that your thoughts and feelings were *valid*.

Another important formula (a three-part calculation) to learn is this:

Thoughts + Feelings = Responses

Responses x *(repeated practice)* = Behavioral Pattern

Behavioral Pattern x *(repeated practice)* = Settled Attitude

You're probably wondering how the 20 percent keep their attitudes on all of the different factors pristine; how they keep from practicing the wrong attitudes. It's simple, but not easy. There is one part of the process that they focus on and scrutinize carefully, but it's not the one you think it is. Your first guess would be that they carefully monitor their thoughts—and to some degree, they do—but have you ever tried *not* to think about something? If I placed a coffee mug in front of you and said, "Don't think about this coffee mug," what would happen? That's right; you'd fixate on it. You wouldn't be able to get it out of your mind.

I mentioned I play golf. If you have ever played a golf hole with a lake in front of the green, you have, no doubt, done what I'm about to describe or know someone who did. The golfer—let's call him Bob—steps up to the tee and says to himself...

"Oh no...there's that lake. I really don't want to hit my shot in the water. I have a good round going on. I'm just not going to think about the lake. I've been hitting the ball well today. The lake isn't going to be a problem if I hit my 7 iron solidly. I just won't think about the darn lake. Don't think about it, Bob. But...I don't want to lose my new golf ball, so I'm going to use an old one just in case. Don't think about the lake. Put it out of you mind, Bob!"

What do you suppose Bob is thinking about when he takes that swing? How does he feel when he reaches into his bag and pulls that old, scuffed-up ball? What is his self-talk causing him to fixate on? Where do you think Bob's ball winds up?

The 20 percent don't waste their time trying to control the myriad of thoughts that fly into their heads. They know it's not possible. They monitor the thoughts, but focus on the *feelings*. When a negative or destructive thought enters their minds, sure, they recognize it, but focus on the feeling it generates. Pros don't try to play thought police with their own heads. They know that thoughts of all kinds are going to run rampant in their minds. They simply take the following three-step process:

1. When a negative or destructive thought enters their minds, they *monitor* it, ask what factors might be driving it.
2. If the thought begins to produce an unproductive *feeling*, they ask themselves the following two questions:
   a. Can I *trust* this feeling?
   b. Will a *response* to this feeling get me to my stated goals?

If the answer is no, they then take step #3:

3. They backtrack to the *source* of the feeling (the thought that generated it) and they *replace* it with an appropriate thought and feeling that will be productive to them.

This is how the self-talk would sound if we joined the conversation in the heads of the 20 percent:

"I know it's only 1:30 in the afternoon, and I should try to set a few more appointments, but I should just go home. This just isn't working for me today."

"Wait…I need to take a deep breath and analyze what's really going on. I know how to prospect and sell. Sure, I'm in a slump, my closing ratio nosedive might be a result of being off my game a little, but that's easy to fix. I'm going to text my manager, Julie, and ask her for some time tomorrow morning so we can work on this together. In the meantime, I have four more hours of prime selling time to set a few more appointments, and I have some warm leads out in this area. I'm going to put the four hours in, let the numbers play out, and I'll fix what's wrong in the morning."

The 20 percent know that thoughts of all kinds might pop into their brains just before important calls or appointments. They know that negative thoughts might creep into their coconuts just after a "No" or a rejection. They don't waste time or energy trying to block them all out. They focus their attention on the feelings and then backtrack to the root thoughts and replace them with productive thoughts, feelings, and behaviors—the ones they've committed to.

That's what the 20 percent do. They know that all feelings can't be trusted. They don't respond to all of them; they carefully monitor them. This is the single greatest edge they have over the rest of their competitors.

Let's go back to the definition of attitude in chapter 14 one last time... let's look at it again and analyze it carefully...

"A settled way of *thinking* or *feeling* about something, typically one that is reflected in a person's *behavior.*"

Elite performers have negative thoughts and feelings, also. They also have slumps; they just don't allow themselves to feel or respond the way the 80 percent do. They take *control* of the process; they backtrack, take a deep breath, and return to their settled way of thinking. They get back on track quickly, and the wins start coming. They are true professionals and will not allow themselves to succumb to destructive thoughts, feelings, or responses of any kind. It's not in their DNA.

The good news about all of this is that most of the 20 percent were not born with silver spoons in their mouths or all this wisdom in their heads. I sure as heck wasn't. They didn't wake up one day suddenly discovering that the sales fairy had delivered them all of the winning tools. Their solid Competencies and winning Attitudes were hard earned. They created their own DNA.

This part of The CAP Equation©—what's explained in the next few chapters—came hard for me. It took years for me to master the process of shifting away from faulty thought processes. Once I began reading great books, it became easier; once I began modeling top producers, it became clearer.

In the chapters that round out this section on Attitudes, we will illuminate the key thought processes that professionals adopt as their language of success. These next two chapters might hold the most distilled, sales-specific content you'll ever see in print, in one place.

Put your seatbelt on.

CHAPTER 16

Million-Dollar Mind-Sets—I

*Commitment Objective
and Engagement Phases*

*"There is one quality which one must possess to win, and
that is definiteness of purpose, the knowledge of what
one wants, and a burning desire to possess it."*

—**NAPOLEON HILL,** American author,
pioneer of personal success movement

So far, I've offered you some truths to chew on. We've discussed that
you'll surely become a product of what you read (your input) and

whom you associate with and model. I've pointed out that successful sales-people all around you leave deep ruts in the road for you to follow. I have proffered the notion that a possible impediment to your success might be your unwillingness to change. We've also explored the hypothesis that you should not trust all of your feelings.

If you have adopted these ideas as engines of truth regarding the formation of Attitudes, then you are ready to add the fuel that will propel you to the other side. The specific Attitudes we explore will be categorized corresponding to phases of maturity in your sales career; however, I'd like to note that it doesn't matter when you commit to developing these Attitudes. You can reengineer and transform your sales career at any time. This is simply a logical way to think of them.

COMMITMENT OBJECTIVE PHASE (Ground Zero)

The Commitment Objective Phase happens when you make your decision to become involved in commission sales. Ideally, this would be the time that you establish a mind-set for the long haul. Waiting too long to determine your foundational Attitudes will only lessen your odds of survival. We'd like to see your mind-sets centered on the key words in this section. These word prompts and philosophies should be examined vigilantly so that you can form strong Attitudes around them. They will support your cause and put you in a position to win.

PURPOSE

You have to know *why* you are doing this thing called commission sales. The 20 percent have a clear understanding of why they are working so hard. Using this key word, you are charged with examining your true purpose for becoming involved in commission sales. Your purpose then becomes your driving force, and if strong enough, can keep you in the game when things get a little cloudy.

I have found that very few salespeople actually know *why* they do what they do, and by "why" I don't mean to make money. That's an outcome or a result, not a purpose. If you go deeper, you'd have to ask what the money would mean to you, what would you do with it, how would it change your life. In other words, what's your *purpose* or *cause*? What are your core beliefs, and why do you roll out of bed in the morning? And finally, *why* should anyone give a crap? **People don't buy *what* you do; they buy *why* you do it.**

I absolutely love what Steve Jobs' thoughts were on this particular subject. He was commenting on both his vision and his purpose when he said:

> "Being the richest man in the cemetery doesn't matter to me. Going to bed at night saying, 'We've done something wonderful,' that's what matters to me."

VISION (What You Wish to Build and Become)

Your vision is different than your purpose. It's the *what* you wish to build or become; *where* you wish to end up.

The 80 percent only see what's in front of them. The 20 percent determine what their incremental and finished products will look like. They have a clear vision of where they will be after year one, year two, and year five. They know exactly what they want to create. It's especially important to have this kind of strong vision in a job that doesn't usually define one for you. Most new salespeople are handed a blank chalkboard—it overwhelms them; it's too vague. The 20 percent know what they want. They visualize it in 3D. They live it, smell it, touch it, and feel it.

If, in your vision, you are driving a different car, then go get a picture of that very car and plaster it on your refrigerator. If you want to earn a certain amount during your first year, then write yourself a personal check in that very amount and tape it to your bathroom mirror. Keep the vision of what you wish to become in sharp focus and in front of you. The 20 percent have such a convincing and magnetic vision that it pulls them through the fog of the battlefield. Develop an attitude of expectation about what you wish to build and become.

FAITH AND CONFIDENCE

Faith is generally defined as complete trust or confidence in someone or something. Faith happens without a lot of immediate evidence. You might recall that we mentioned early on in this book that life happens looking forward but can only truly be understood looking backward.

The 80 percent often reveal their massive insecurities. They've not acquired the entire set of core Competencies needed; hence, their confidence level is low. As their gas tanks get even lower, they are less prone to adopt the type of attitudes we are talking about.

The 20 percent have total faith in their Competencies because they've drilled and rehearsed them. They also have confidence in the Attitudes they've settled on. They have mastered the way they choose to think, feel, and respond. They have selected a mentor or two whom they can latch onto. They know it's going to happen; they're quietly confident.

You've heard the phrase, *fake it till you make it.* Why don't we replace that saying with, *faith it till you make it.* The 20 percent have faith in themselves, their mentors, and their system. Faith allows a person to become committed.

COMMITMENT

This area would seem unnecessary to discuss—except for the known fact that most new salespeople enter the game with one foot in and one foot out. I can't tell you how many times I've caught a new salesperson saying things like, "I'm *hoping* this thing works out for me," or "I'm going to give this thing a *try*." Sheesh! Neither of those two verbalized positions will result in career success in sales.

The 20 percent are completely committed to their business and the work that must be done to reach their stated goals. They make a *solemn promise* to do everything in their power to succeed. They burn the bridge and cast off the lifeboats. It's that serious and that important that you are truly committed. Cultivate an Attitude rooted in commitment.

DETERMINATION (You Can't Fail if You Don't Quit)

Love that saying! You've heard it before, right? Babe Ruth said: "It's hard to beat someone who won't quit."

At the end of the day, the Bambino was right, and this is the truth. However, a fierce level of determination, the kind of resolve that keeps you in the game until you start winning, isn't possible until a person has a strong purpose, a clear vision, and unwavering faith. The reflex to keep on stumbling forward, even after you've been kicked in the teeth, won't click in if purpose, vision, and faith aren't in evidence. Determination *follows* these three other attitudes. It does not precede them.

ENGAGEMENT PHASE (Days 1–30)

This is where your decision to become a commission salesperson merges with the effort that you'll have to expend and the knowledge you will have to absorb to gain your Competencies. This is the phase of the business where you roll up your sleeves and get your hands dirty, setting your first appointments, giving your first presentations. You are jumping into the water.

TAKING INSTRUCTION (Listening and Applying)

All top performers embrace Attitudes that help them receive information fruitfully; they open their receptors and don't block or prejudge the message or the messenger. They trust both until there is a good reason not to. They seek out any and all available training and instruction and begin to internalize it. In fact, if they don't think there is enough education, they ask for more.

I've often used the example of what happens when you're strapping yourself in on a commercial flight, when the helpful flight attendant explains the safety features of the airplane. They are instructing us on procedures that could potentially save our lives, but nobody's listening. We're all staring at our mobile devices, taking out our reading materials, or trying to find a pillow. A psychologist would tell us that we don't listen to them because we subconsciously regard the information as unimportant to us at that precise moment.

But what if the flight attendant started their address with, "Ladies and gentlemen, the captain has informed me that one of our engines sounds a little funny and the landing gear is sticking." Would she have your attention then?

Think of the instruction and training you're being offered as potentially life saving. From a financial standpoint, it is, unless you are a trust fund baby.

The 80 percent sometimes interrupt the person coaching them, interjecting their own ideas. People that are failing think they know everything. Conversely, top producers are always eager to learn. They want to know what actually works. They prefer to be prepared before going into battle, and they know that their coach or trainer has been there. The 20 percent know that while it's great to learn through experience, it's even better to learn through somebody else's experience.

PEER-TO-PEER RELATIONSHIPS
(The People You Associate With)

Smart, new salespeople seek out top producers and mentors to build relationships with. These budding superstars choose their accomplices wisely. They aren't jealous of top producers or management. They hold nobody in contempt. They want to know what the best of the best in their business are thinking, feeling, and doing regarding the same issues they are dealing with.

THE WORK (Paying Your Dues)

All top producers I've ever met have an accommodating attitude about the initial and ongoing work that has to be done. They adopt a "whatever it takes" mentality in order to learn the skills necessary to succeed. They prepare to work twice as hard as might be suggested. The 80 percent have no idea what the dues are. The 20 percent have paid their dues and are still paying them. They get it. The 20 percent simply do the work.

The necessary commitment to the work hit me somewhere after my first year with Penn Life. I knew I could make a decent living strolling down the street selling accident policies. I'd worked hard on my skills and could get my numbers in and still be at the municipal golf course by 3:30 p.m. to play a quick nine. Life was good. I was even starting to slack off a little.

Then my manager conned me into training people. "Just take a few guys with you and show them what you do. It's easy," he told me. Of course, it wasn't easy, and it involved more than he was letting on. They wanted to suck me in slowly and then promote me to a formal management level. They put pressure on me until I caved in. So, there I was...an accomplished young salesperson, yet needing to go back to square one again and learn a brand new set of skills.

I spent the next year learning how to recruit and train salespeople. It was painful, but I figured things out through trial and error. I was willing to stumble forward and get bloody. My personal production and income suffered initially as I focused on others, but I stayed the course and eventually things began to balance out. That's how it works. You pump the pump over and over again and no water comes out, then a trickle, and then a gush.

By March of '82, I'd been in sales for about three years. At that juncture, I was a darn good salesperson and an even better sales trainer and recruiter. I had skills that were transferable to almost any other industry or market. I'd been averaging sixty-five-hour workweeks if you aggregated all my time selling, recruiting, training, drilling, rehearsing, reading books, and picking brains. Those 156 weeks multiplied by 65 hours equaled 10,140 hours.

I have referred to "your 10,000 hours," but allow me to expand on it. In Malcolm Gladwell's third book, *Outliers: The Story of Success*, he scrutinizes factors that contribute to high levels of success. Throughout the publication, Gladwell repeatedly mentions the "10,000-Hour Rule," claiming the key to success in any field is, to a great extent, a matter of practicing a specific task for a total of around 10,000 hours. His book was well received by most, yet Gladwell was criticized for oversimplifying success. It really doesn't matter whether you completely subscribe to Gladwell's philosophy or not, but I'm a simple guy, so his hypothesis resonated with me. What I took away from the book was that I actually practiced my way to success.

What I also took away was that if you aren't naturally smart (and I'm not), and if you don't have a fancy degree (which I don't), and if you don't come from wealth (and I didn't), you better be willing to pay your dues. Hence, decades before Gladwell wrote about it, I put in my 10,000 hours. I paid my dues.

So, what did my initial 10,000 hours with Penn Life buy me? Options. Relative freedom. If I had circulated my resume at that time, there'd have been a dozen organizations beating a path to my door. I'd bought career options with my 10,000 hours. I was battle hardened. I'd developed the ability to self-assess and self-correct using the emotional intelligence amassed from so many hours in the game. I didn't need anyone to hold my hand anymore.

During this time, I was paying close attention to the obvious separation between those who make it in sales and those who do not. The most obvious disparity was (and still is) the divergent attitudes about *the work* itself. The 20 percent were perpetually hungry—always willing to do the work, put in the hours, pay the cost. The 80 percent *say* they want success, but don't *pay* their dues. Conversely, the 20 percent pay their dues without question and are willing to continue paying them to get to the next level.

More than simply putting in the hours, the 20 percent also seemed to *honor* the work. What I mean by "honor" is that they respect the work. They want to be the best presenter, closer, and so on. They want to become an ultimate professional. This desire to be excellent transcends earning commission for them. Oh, don't get me wrong, they want to earn a great deal of money, but they have tremendous pride in what they do. They not only want to earn big money, they want to be recognized as the best at what they do. The 80 percent? Not so much. They're often not focused on the quality of their work. I guess you can say they go through the motions, and then they ask, "When's the big money coming?" They're not willing to make their work excellent; they simply don't respect it like the 20 percent do.

What side of this fence do you sit on?

If you are new in sales and are verbalizing that you want to be a top producer, are you willing to put in your 10,000 hours? Are you a seasoned salesperson who's stuck? Are you ready to recommit, put in more hours so that you can get to the next level, possibly even become financially free?

There were two other times in my sales leadership career—after I thought most of the hard work and learning curve were over—that I had to make the decision to commit to another 10,000 hours. The most significant one of those two times was when I accepted a high-level, sales-management role with Aflac in October of 1995. For the first time in my career, I was going to be leading leaders and coaching coaches. I was also going to be responsible for many other areas of an agency business model. That complex role forced me into the admission that I needed some help, some additional mentorship. Also, there would be another 10,000 hours.

The most current incarnation of my 10,000 hours began when I woke up one morning recently and decided to reinvent myself, to become an author, sales and leadership trainer, and national speaker. I don't know much about this new industry yet, but I do know this—my 10,000 hours needs to be put in all over again. I'll get beat up a little for sure, but trust me, I'll figure this game out just like I did the last one and the one before that. I'll develop the competencies needed and adopt the attitudes required to propel myself forward. I know the formula.

The difference between me and some others is that I'm happily willing to pay the cost, once again—another 10,000 hours. I want to climb to the top of my new industry, and I know what the price is. I'm willing to pay the toll to be excellent at what I do. Is this how you feel?

PERSONAL RESPONSIBILITY
(Owning Your Actions and Results)

Sometimes, a new business or industry is tough to get traction in, tough to succeed in. Sometimes, a slow local or national economy can hinder your progress. These are market realities. Ultimately, however, the market conditions are the same for everyone in the game.

So what's my point? Often, I've seen salespeople failing or struggling in organizations. They're pointing fingers at everyone and everything else around them. "This job is just too hard," they tell their managers. They pontificate that the salespeople that are succeeding are lucky, were given better leads, or assigned a more favorable territory. "These products are just too hard to sell," they snap. "I quit!" They put in their resignation and they're gone.

We hire another salesperson. We place her on the same team; enroll her in the same training school; she reports to the same manager and works the same territory; she sells the same products to the same target prospects; she becomes successful. So, if you are following this tale, one person quits, saying, "This thing doesn't work," just to have someone else step into the very same position and do extremely well, even become wealthy over a period of time.

Unfortunately, I've seen this odd little scenario play out far too often. What do you think the difference between these two examples, these two salespeople, is? If you answered that the second salesperson exercised a level of "personal responsibility" over her career, then please go to the head of the class.

Take ownership of your actions and results going into your position. Resist the urge to point fingers and create blame for your lack of production. The person responsible for your lack of growth will always be the person staring back at you when you look in the mirror. If somebody else is making it, you can, too. The market conditions are the same for everybody.

CHAPTER 17

Million-Dollar
Mind-Sets—II

Development and Evolution Phases

"Failure is not fatal, but failure to change might be."

—**JOHN WOODEN,** legendary UCLA basketball coach

As you venture deeper, into the first few months of your commission sales career, you will experience emotions you never dreamed possible—good and bad. You will encounter small obstacles, some easy enough to step around. You will also encounter big walls, ones that seem insurmountable to negotiate. It is then that the Attitudes explored in this chapter become so important. The people that stick and stay in this game will settle on and practice the Attitudes described, the rest will not.

Let's examine the critical mind-sets that should be developed during the next two phases of your career:

DEVELOPMENT PHASE (Months Two – Six)

This phase usually begins after your first month of intensive field experience. Once you get a few bumps and bruises under your belt, you can start to gain a level of maturity in your thought process about sales. There are a few weighty belief systems that must be established during this time. The Attitudes that elite performers build around the key words below will allow you to run the race without crashing and burning psychologically or emotionally.

EMOTIONAL CONTROLS (Running Level)

A common trait of superstars is that they never allow themselves to get too high or too low. They live in the middle; they run level. You can't tell whether they had a good day or bad. They can do this because they know their market and have their presentation and closing skills down cold. They know how the numbers work—they know the formula. As a result, they carry a high level of confidence into the field. They are calm, cool, and collected. You may hear about crazy salespeople, but if they are truly nuts, they don't last.

When professionals are selling, they are usually in the zone, on autopilot. They know what to say and how to say it. They don't get nervous. They might be anxious, but they've performed the tasks so many times that they allow instinct to take over; they stay the course. They already know what the results will be. Everything is predictable to them. The top 20 percent take the pressure off their own backs and put it on the system. This allows them to run level and run for a long time.

BENCHMARKS (Celebrating Small Victories)

Top producers know that success is made up of a series of small victories. The pros know that these small victories happen each day if you are looking for them. Conversely, struggling, new salespeople are looking for that one big break. They are chasing the big deal that's going to jumpstart their careers and put them on the map. They are not satisfied benchmarking their successes through predictable wins. One of my mentors (and also one of my favorite people in the world), a man named Jimmy Hill, used to say:

> "When you're new, make sure you're shooting a lot of rabbits, not hunting elephants. If an elephant walks into your sights, take a shot; just don't set out to hunt them."

Of course, "rabbits" represent the small victories that eventually lead to larger ones. You can always feed your family when you shoot rabbits. "Elephants" refer to larger, more complex targets, markets, or prospects. These are harder to gain access to and close. Elephants have long sales cycles. A new salesperson can easily starve to death trying to bag an elephant! Don't chase elephants. Collect small victories and create momentum!

EXECUTION (Selecting and Implementing Strategies)

Elite performers are all about execution. Pros select only a few proven strategies and then implement those few methods well. They might occasionally abandon projects when they see that further effort is fruitless, but they can do that because they've developed a decent instinct. Pros begin and finish their projects and initiatives. They don't allow the whirlwind to distract them from the priorities they've chosen to tackle.

Amateurs are quite a different story. What we've found over the years is that amateurs have *lots* of great ideas and grandiose plans, but rarely accomplish any of them.

FAILURE AND REJECTION (Reframing Technique)

We visit this philosophy again in a slightly different format when we arrive at our study of Pipeline practices; however, I also want to touch on this failure/rejection practice in this chapter (as an Attitude) because it should become a cornerstone outlook if you plan to survive and thrive in commission sales.

A settled Attitude regarding how to reframe failure and rejection can only be formed once you have developed an acceptable CAP Score© on most of your core Competencies. Let's assume you've become competent, and as a result, confident in your abilities. We will also assume that you've learned how your numbers work; you know your conversion ratios. At this point, you can then adopt the Attitude we are going to describe and it will let you stay enthusiastically involved in your activities and shift all the pressure onto the system. This philosophy is *magic* when learned, adopted, and applied properly.

This is how it works. Pros automatically relabel and reframe failure and rejection.

Failure—There's no such thing as *failure* to a pro. To them, failure would only truly occur if they quit or stopped working. While the 80 percent might "fail" to set an appointment with a key prospect, the 20 percent simply haven't determined how to gain access yet. While amateurs "fail" to walk out with a contract, "fail" at closing the sale, the pro leaves with an expected metric result to be analyzed later, after the workday is over.

Rejection—To a pro, *rejection* doesn't exist, either. A lead can't logically or truly "reject" you or your message if they are not willing to sit down and discuss it; they're simply not open-minded to a meeting. It's never personal, and pros choose not to attach any emotional value to the lead's response.

The 80 percent get a "No," followed by a blow-off, followed by a prospect standing them up, followed by someone who won't even see them, and they tend to view all of this as negative. The 20 percent don't process it that way. While the amateurs are disappointed, even feeling like they've flopped, the pros have already settled on very different ways of managing this. To them, all responses from prospects fit into only one neat category: the 20 percent see all responses as simply *metric results.*

Pros know that a certain percentage of their presentations will result in a predictable percentage of wins and losses. They know that each dial or cold call will not result in an appointment. They understand the numbers and know they have to let the numbers play out. They are simply taking their cuts at the plate, and they are pleased if they meet or exceed their expected conversion ratios.

I was sitting with Jack Canfield discussing The CAP Equation© as he told a story about a salesperson who was telemarketing for one of his programs. Typically, one out of nine calls converted into a sale. He mentioned that this poor sales guy went eighty-one calls without a sale, which was unheard of. Then, they watched as the same salesperson closed the next eight in a row, which was also unheard of. Jack and I had a good laugh over this, because we both got it. That professional salesperson was simply playing out his string; he knew the eighty-one "Nos" were simply a *metric result* of continuing to do the right things. He knew that the "Yes's" would eventually come, and they'd come in bunches.

This settled Attitude about reframing failure and rejection allows you to assimilate all responses without wasted emotion and label them as something that is neutral versus something negative that can begin to erode your energy or poise.

Peak performers register a "No" and they move along as if nothing unusual happened. Adopting this philosophy allows them to make another call and another, until their Pipelines are overflowing with wins. They will analyze their results in volume, not individually.

Value of Time

This is different than *time management*. Valuing your time is about what's really important to *you* and how you are going to support it in your life. We spent some time on this concept in chapter 3, and I told you that the management and valuation of your precious time was both a Competency and an Attitude. It can even play a big part of how you manage your Pipeline. This multifaceted area simply crosses over all three components of The CAP Equation©.

What I will challenge you to do in this area is begin to think about your time, broken down into three different silos. I want you to develop a focused approach to using your time. This is something I took away from my personal time with Jack Canfield, also, and I have adapted the practice to my personal calendar. Let me break these down and describe them in the following sections.

WORK TIME/DAYS

Work time and workdays are demarcated intervals that you have carefully set aside in your calendar for productive work and nothing else. Once these times are established, you should allow nothing more than a family emergency to alter your course.

When you work, you work. Be selfish. Say "No" if you have to. This is your time to work. This is the time you have established to prospect, present, facilitate, offer service, and ask for referrals. Period. Nothing else.

BUFFER TIME/DAYS

While work time is a fixed period of time that allows you to focus solely on your career, buffer time is the time that you can set aside in your calendar to take care of the things that are important to attend to in your life. These are tasks and errands that, if not attended to, could cause an imbalance that could eventually affect your health, career, or family stability.

Examples of what you would schedule into buffer time might be any appointment that would be health related, such as a routine physical, dental, or vision check-up. Other less weighty buffer time errands can include hair or beauty appointments, dropping off your clothes at the cleaners, or picking up groceries for the week. Buffer time should also be used for the important opportunities, such as going to your child's soccer game or debate club event as well as taking the kids back and forth to school or their appointments.

Your goal should be to *group* these types of activities and errands together as much as possible so that when you are scheduling buffer time in your calendar, you're packing as much of these *same* type of actions into the block of time you have set aside for them. You will not be an effective salesperson if you are prospecting for an hour, and then stopping by the pub to get a beer, then making calls for another forty-five minutes, then running to pick up your dry cleaning.

Just as you demarcate time for *work* and nothing else, you should also establish focused *buffer* time and fit as many of these activities into that time as possible. If you begin doing this, your stress will go down and your productivity will go up.

FREE DAYS

This is the tough one. Free days are simply that. *Free*. They are free from work-related issues and free from stress. You *unplug*. You leave your phone in your desk drawer at home if you can. You don't discuss work or career issues with your spouse or significant other. You choose activities that refresh you and allow you to reboot. You focus solely on those things that you have chosen to do and you stay *present* for the people you are with. I know...this is going to take some work for some of us—including me—but let's make a commitment to work on it together.

EVOLUTION PHASE (Second Six Months)

The next phase of growth typically occurs between your seventh to twelfth months in the business. We'll call it *the zone*. This is where you know most of what you need to know to make a living. This is a time when you will also need even more mentors and fellowship to keep your head above water. This is a stage where things can go really bad in a hurry if you don't have your head screwed on tight.

HUMILITY

Mediocre salespeople boast when they close something or have a good week. The 20 percent are humble. They don't slap themselves on the back and are oftentimes uncomfortable with recognition. They prefer to just smile and let their work do the talking.

I have seen many a salesperson have early success. Early wins are awesome; however, they might result in a great deal of recognition for the salesperson from the organization they work for. Now don't get me wrong; acknowledgment from hierarchy and peers isn't a bad thing; it can actually serve as great nourishment. But what happens when a person reads his or her own press clippings *is* a bad thing. The problems begin when they start to believe that they have *arrived* and no further learning or growth is necessary. Their false sense of arrival or accomplishment can block them, shut off their desire to acquire more tools. After this, a death spiral is inevitable. It's hard to watch. Be humble at all times!

FOCUS (Avoiding Distractions)

Elite performers practice single-mindedness on all of the right things, the priorities of their business. They don't get sucked into sidebar distractions or politics in their office or around them. They don't gaze at shiny objects or try to spread themselves too thin. They know how to say "No" to opportunities that look good on the surface but will take them away from their core Competencies and their prime-earning potential. The 20 percent know they can't do everything. They want to become great at only a handful of things.

There are two scenarios that can distract a salesperson during their first year: too little success or too much success. If they are not producing up to their minimum goal, they can become stressed and take their eyes off the ball, stop doing what's necessary to fight through the wall. It's easy to lose yourself when you're stumbling.

Surprisingly, it's even easier to lose focus when you're succeeding. (See "Humility," above.) An over celebratory attitude can foster arrogance and false confidence, and a person can slow or stop prospecting and growing.

People who are on their way to being the 20 percent don't let distractions, politics, or levels of success deter them from their planned work activities. They focus on the work.

These are the most vital of the million-dollar mind-sets you'll need to develop and practice to survive your first year in sales. These Attitudes must be adopted and added to your core, hard-wired, Competencies. When you add these first two components of The CAP Equation© together, it becomes magical. It lays the foundation for you to become wealthy in sales.

There is one last component of The CAP Equation©. This one is the multiplier. Like my old friend, John, explained to me at the chilidog stand that day in 1980, if they're saying the *right things* in the *right way* and they're still failing, they're probably not saying them to *enough people.*

PART IV

Pipeline $- C + A \times P$

CHAPTER 18

Pipeline–I

The Multiplier

"Two things you can control: The quality and frequency of your message."
—**JOHN KALENCH,** author, sales trainer

Your Pipeline is the lifeblood of your business and income. When you properly multiply the qualified leads in your Pipeline by the combination of your Competencies and Attitudes, anything other than unlimited success in sales is impossible. *Game over*!

Of course, the opposite is true also. You can fully develop all of the core Competencies, manifest all of the key Attitudes, but as the man said, if you don't see enough of the right people, you are going to crash and burn anyway. All three of the components are interdependent on each other for the equation to work.

In the next two chapters we are going to discuss the third and final component of The CAP Equation©. We will teach you how to keep the vitality of your business flowing. We show you how to manage your Pipeline so that failure becomes impossible.

I have found that many top salespeople think in terms of pictures. Let me reference the Pipeline image I've always kept in my mind. (Pictured on the previous page) It is a series of horizontal pipes fitted together—larger end to smaller end—like a telescope. I have always visualized my job as that of loading raw leads into the fat part of my Pipeline as fast and hard as I could. I viewed the practice as a manufacturing process. I would refine—continue working—the raw leads, until one of two things occurred: the lead stalled (flawed material) or the lead converted—I manufactured a *win*.

Along the way of this "manufacturing process," I would attach logical titles for the lead categories as they moved through different sections of my Pipeline. Of course, you can attach any name that works for you; however, I chose the following labels:

- **Universe/Raw Lead**—Leads that fit your broadest definition of "targets"
- **Targets**–A lead that you are in the process of qualifying
- **Suspects**–A Lead that's qualified to the extent that you wish to call on it
- **Prospects/Qualified**—A set appointment or one in the presentation phase
- **Proposals**—Presentation given, follow-up phase (between "no" and "yes")
- **Win**—This is a "yes"

My practice was to jam as many raw leads as I could into the large end, track them carefully, and envision my Pipeline exploding from the pressure of the volume. Once I got the hang of filling and keeping the Pipeline full, my commission flow became steady, just like a regular paycheck.

Let's begin to break down the key Pipeline practices that you need to identify, learn, and commit to habit.

RAW-LEAD VOLUME—X 2

Does this look familiar? We discussed this concept as part of your prospecting Competencies. If you recall, we asked you to consider loading as much raw- lead material as possible into your Pipeline. We urged you to load *twice* the number of raw leads you think you might need into your Pipeline. Turn on any and all lead spigots you have access to. Don't worry yet about qualifying your lead sources as good or bad. Let's simply get all of the leads jammed into your Pipeline until it's overflowing. You can sort things out later.

If the organization you're part of told you that you need one hundred leads to get started, then load two hundred into your Pipeline. If the company you work with told you to get two hundred leads, then go load four hundred into your Pipeline. *Double* what they tell you!

The reason that you should do this might not be immediately obvious to you. Think about it—if you have *twice* the number of raw leads in your Pipeline that they tell you to have, how would that change the way you feel? Would you become more relaxed? Would you naturally be more confident? Would you be more eager and excited to dig in to the vast pile of leads?

If you have only one hundred leads, you'll be more protective of them, almost like they are sacred and you need them to last. If you have four hundred leads, you don't care as much. You'll be less protective of them. You'll have a natural tendency to want to get through them faster. Lastly, you will want to get to a "No" as quickly as possible so that you can get to the next lead. This one strategy is so simple that it, alone, can alter a person's path in sales. It's a Jedi mind trick, but it's magic when applied.

MULTIPLE LEAD SOURCES (Spigots)

I've asked you to turn on all lead sources/spigots and load your Pipeline as fully as possible. It is never a great bet to have only one lead source. You can live by that one source, but you can also die by it. For the logical sake of Pipeline stability, you would be wise to have multiple sources.

During your first six to twelve months, we want you to try it all. We want you to open all lead spigots possible. While this is a good practice at first, at some point (usually after your flow of *wins* are sufficient), it might make sense for you to begin to assess your lead sources and identify where your highest ROI is coming from—geographically and demographically. You will also want to be aware of where your lead-generation efforts are going unrewarded.

My bet is that 80 percent of your best, qualified leads are coming from only 20 percent of your sources/efforts. (Have you heard of this 80-20 rule before?) My suggestion is for you to begin to shift more of your efforts and resources away from low-ROI sources and redirect them toward the high-ROI sources. Hence, after you've been at this a while, make sure you evaluate which spigots are pumping out high-ROI leads and which are not. Then, simply prime the lead spigots that are most fruitful and reduce time spent in the other areas.

SHORT-CYCLE TARGETS (Low-Hanging Fruit)

We briefly touched on this earlier when we studied Competencies. After you transition into your third month in the field, I suggest that you apply the same analysis we described above, to your *wins*. Take a look at your closed deals, the ones that closed fast, and ask the following questions:

- Do they have any similarity to each other?
- What size or price point were they?
- Were they from a certain demographic or geographic area?
- What market conditions made them easy to close?

What you're looking for is *low-hanging fruit*. These are the most fertile prospects, the types that close the quickest. The point here is to be mindful that you are still in the critical-momentum phase of the business, and it's better to shoot a lot of rabbits and eat than go elephant hunting and starve.

SUSTAINED PROSPECTING FLOW

You simply cannot stop the flow in your Pipeline for any reason. There is no good reason, but trust me, I've heard all of the excuses for doing so. There are two common reasons new salespeople stop prospecting and setting appointments. I believe we touched on them earlier in the book; however, it is important to revisit and reinforce why you want to avoid these faulty thought processes. I simply don't want you to fall victim to them.

REASON #1—TOO MUCH SUCCESS

It's not uncommon for new salespeople who have experienced a few early wins to stop prospecting and setting appointments. The reasons they will sabotage their lead flow are typically twofold:

1. *Overconfidence (Arrogance)*

Let's join the conversation that's going on in Bob's head:

"I just closed four deals in my first month. Nobody else who started when I did has closed more than one. This sales thing is pretty easy for me because I'm so good. I'm cleaning the floor with the rest of my sales class. I'm going to be the guy up on stage getting the awards this quarter. And the commission...I can already taste it. Hey, I don't really need to cold call this week; I'm going to cruise a little, enjoy this rush of success, and maybe even take Thursday off. Life is good!"

Life might be good for Bob at this point, but if he doesn't check himself, he's going to wreck himself. Ill explain why after we crawl inside of Julie's head.

2. *Fear (How to handle all that business)*

Julie has a very different reason for crimping her air hose. Let's listen in to her inner dialogue:

> "Wow, I never thought I'd have this much success this fast. I'm overwhelmed. I have people jumping into my program, and I'm not sure I can handle all of this. I better stop calling on new prospects. I just don't think I can handle what I've already got sold. Yeah, that's the right idea...I'll just chill out on the prospecting for now until my desk is clear."

Not the right idea at all, Julie. The much better idea would be to keep prospecting and ask for help from your hierarchy. Let's look at the only other reason that new salespeople stop prospecting.

Reason #2—Too Little Success

Some new salespeople who don't experience early success have a tendency to slow or stop their prospecting and appointment-setting efforts. Let's explore the two most common triggers that result in this conscious or unconscious choice:

1. *Confusion (Classroom and field conflict)*

Let's join the conversation in Julie's head:

> "I really enjoyed our sales training at the home office and the online modules, but as I get out here in the field, I've noticed that my manager has a totally different way of approaching people. His front talk is completely different than what we were taught. It seems to work for his quirky personality, and he wants me to do it 'his way,' but I don't think I can pull it off. I'm just so confused. I'm not having any success at all, and I don't want to call on people because I'm not sure what to even say to them. I'm simply not going to make any more calls right now."

Unfortunately, the scenario that Julie is experiencing is far from rare. Confusion, not lack of desire, is holding her back, and who can blame her.

2. *Empty Tank (Going the wrong way/not willing to ask for direction)*

Okay, one last time in Bob's head. Let's listen in:

"I'm not sure that this business works. I went to their training, listened to what they had to say, but hey, I know how to sell, I've been selling for years. I know how to prospect and get an appointment. I wrote my own approach script. But, maybe I'm doing something wrong, maybe I should ask for help. Nah...how would it look if an experienced salesperson, like me, went to that young guy who manages me and asked for help. I'm sure it's not me. These programs are just too hard to sell in this local market."

That's right, Bob, it's not you; it's your ego. Bob had horrible results because he did things his way and they didn't work. The end result is that he also stopped prospecting.

If at any time, for any reason, you choose to stop prospecting and generating qualified appointments, you are dead in the water. The result will eventually be an empty Pipeline; however, you won't feel it at first. It will be a *deferred* penalty. At the thirty-day mark, your Pipeline will slow, and somewhere between sixty and ninety days, it will become empty. Then, you will have to prime the pump all over again and experience even more pain, just as if it were your first day again. The hard truth is that a lot of salespeople who stop prospecting at some point during their first year don't survive.

If you are having too *much* success and become overconfident, like Bob, check yourself and understand that your success and the subsequent recognition will all be short-lived. If you close some deals early on and become overwhelmed, like Julie, then you need to go upline, to your hierarchy, and ask for help. Your manager should be overjoyed to lend a hand because he or she doesn't want to see you crimp your Pipeline.

If you are experiencing too *little* success, like Julie, because you are confused by what's being taught in the classroom versus the field, by all means, ask for a meeting and work it out. If you have stopped prospecting because your way isn't working—like Bob—maybe you should try it *their way*. Assume they know what they're doing; they've been doing it for awhile and know what works.

Regardless of the reason you have chosen to stop prospecting and generating qualified appointments, *your motivations are faulty*, and they will probably cost you a successful career in sales. *Never* stop prospecting!

CHAPTER 19

Pipeline–II

Conversion Ratios and Metric Results

*"To succeed in sales, simply talk to lots of people every day.
And here's what's exciting–there are lots of people!"*

—JIM ROHN

We spent a little bit of time on conversion ratios earlier in the book; however, this is a practice that is most critical and applicable in the care and feeding of your Pipeline, hence I want to hit this point again.

You must *know* your conversion ratios cold! You have to be able to determine the amount of time you will need to schedule in your calendar to generate enough appointments to reach your stated income goals. You cannot accomplish this if you don't know what your conversion ratios are. Let's break down which conversion ratios you generally need to know.

CONVERSION RATIOS:

RAW LEADS TO QUALIFIED LEADS (Ratio and Time Element)

Determine how many *raw* leads you have to drop into your Pipeline to equal one *qualified* lead and how much time it takes to qualify them. For example: You load thirty raw leads into your Pipeline and you decide that it will take you one hour to *scrub* them (call them or research online) to determine if they're qualified to pursue for a meeting or presentation. You also conclude that in those thirty raw leads, only ten will "scrub out" as qualified and worth pursuing.

QUALIFIED LEADS TO APPOINTMENTS
(Conversion Ratio and Time Element)

This is where you determine what your conversion ratio of qualified leads to appointments is with one or more decision makers. We had an abbreviated discussion on this topic in chapter 8, and I gave the following personal example: When I used the phone to reach qualified prospects, I could make sixty calls per hour. Out of those sixty, I would have a live conversation with six to nine decision makers. Out of those decision makers, two to three would grant me an appointment. Another two to three would show interest but ask me to call back at a later time; the last two to three would express no interest and ask that I not call them back.

As a result of knowing my conversion ratios in this category, I was confident that I could set two to three appointments with decision makers per hour as long as I got my sixty dials in. Of course, some days were better than others, but even on a bad day, I could set one appointment an hour. The important thing to note is that your settled ratios will always even out and hold up over time.

APPOINTMENTS SET TO APPOINTMENTS HELD
(Cancellations/No Shows)

Of course, it's the real world, and not all the appointments you *set* will actually be *held*. Hence, another ratio that you'll have to know will be the fallout rate of scheduled appointments. Simply determine what the reasonable cancellation rate is and factor it in. For example: Traditionally, there is a 20 percent cancelation or no-show rate in our territory. I want to net eight appointments this week; therefore, I will need to schedule ten.

APPOINTMENTS TO SALES

This ratio, of course, is the most critical of conversion metrics from an income standpoint. My suggestion is that you schedule time with your direct manager to review what the closing ratio should be for a person at your level of acumen. I also suggest that you ask your manager what the closing ratio should be after six months and twelve months. You want to have those benchmarks in mind.

Then, knowing your organizational closing average, you need to determine how many closes, deals, or sales you need to make in any given week to pay your bills. Of course, I am making the assumption that you have already figured out what the average commission per sale is in your specific market. Assuming that, let's use this example:

> "The average commission per sale is $1,500. I need to make at least one sale per week to pay my expenses, reserve money for self-employment taxes, and place some small amount in savings. The average closing ratio for a new salesperson here at ABC Company is 20 percent (one out of five). I want to make certain that I have at least five highly qualified appointments with decision makers this week, so I am going to set ten (knowing at least two will not hold up). I will have a net appointment count of eight and 1.5 sales if my closing ratio is industry average."

So, there you have it. In the example above, the salesperson has worked through the conversion ratios and is confident that setting ten appointments will yield enough income to meet the stated goals over the course of the production month and has even built in a small buffer.

A couple of last notes on your conversion ratios. These are simply examples, and I'm sure your needs and metrics will be different, but I think you can see now that knowing these metrics is critical to your ability to schedule time and forecast the work you need to meet your income goals. It is vital that you learn how to backtrack your income needs to these conversion metrics to ensure that you're hard-wiring enough time in your calendar to meet and exceed your stated income goals.

The very last thing I want to remind you of is to keep an eye on *all* of your conversion ratios. If they are weak or suffering (and what I mean by that is they're well below your organization's average), please yell for help. You want to be able to play at a major league level and manage your Pipeline like a pro. Your conversion ratios are a clear indication of your skill levels, and if they're below par, your ability to run your Pipeline is in serious jeopardy.

DRIVING TO A RESULT (Keeping the Pipeline Flowing)

This is a big one! All top producers like to get to a result as quickly as possible. This accomplishes two things for them:

> **#1**—It allows them to close a loop on that lead, register the result, and move on to a fresh lead. It ultimately allows for a much higher volume of leads to travel through their Pipelines; hence, more total *wins* can occur.

> **#2**—A definite result energizes them because they know each quantifiable result places them one step closer to their next "Yes." Having a lot of "Maybes" in the Pipeline clogs it up. Worse, any lead that can't be placed in a definable metric category becomes an energy vampire for salespeople and usually slows their overall activities.

Pros simply hate "Maybes" because they're like quicksand—"Maybe" isn't a classifiable or categorical metric result. You can't throw the lead in the trash just yet, but it isn't shooting out the small end of the Pipeline as a *win* either. A "Maybe" occupies space in your brain and in your calendar without paying any rent. The danger, especially for a new salesperson, is that "Maybe" seems promising. The newbie spends a great deal of time following up—calling back repeatedly—without knowing what the prospect's tangible objection is or why there is a lack of traction.

Once I figured out the sales game, I knew that one of two things would happen to each lead as I called on it. I would either remove it from the production line (my Pipeline), labeling it "flawed material" or it was going to shoot out of the small end of the Pipeline as a *win*!

I knew each of my leads would eventually fall into one of those two result categories, and *only* those two. I knew this because those were the *only* two types of results I would *allow* for in my Pipeline. I did not have any capacity in my Pipeline for a "Maybe." Any Pipeline practice other than this I refer to as "massaging leads." This practice will kill your momentum and Pipeline flow. Massaging leads and chasing "Maybes" has never worked, and it's simply not what pros do!

You must be able to determine why your prospects aren't moving to a "Yes" and try to overcome their objections quickly. If you can't identify one or more specific objections, then you must get them to tell you "No" so that you can kick the prospects out of your Pipeline and clear space for a new, fresh, qualified lead. I know this philosophy might seem counterintuitive, but I'm begging you to get them to say "No" if you can't get a "Yes." I'm aware there's another school of thought on this; however, I'm here to tell you that I've never seen a salesperson thrive that didn't get this concept down cold!

METRIC RESULT PRACTICE

The Metric Result Practice is the big concept that we've been touching on and suggesting throughout this entire book. It fits nicely in this Pipeline chapter, but can also be viewed as an Attitude. I believe it's a lot like the subject of time management, in that it can transcend all three components of The CAP Equation©. Let's review this incredibly important method one more time to make sure that you understand how to apply it.

The Metric Result Practice first starts when you reframe any failure or rejection as simply a result. The practice continues to build on itself when you are willing to aggressively drive a prospect to say, "No." Don't get me wrong; we all like to hear, "Yes"; however, the 20 percent are ultimately okay with a "No" because it's a definite result.

The Metric Result Practice really takes tangible shape when you begin to gain momentum in your Pipeline. When you are driving to results with solid Competencies, you will have a lot of metric data to analyze. The "No" that you just received this morning is another metric result that fits into a measurable category. It can now be tallied and analyzed. It becomes part of the group that predictably *should* say "No." The best part of this practice is that you can smile when you add the "No" to your metrics because you just got paid.

If you think about it, you get paid whether they say "Yes" or "No." You know your standard conversion ratios. In my example earlier, out of five completed presentations, one will say "Yes" and the other four will say "No." Hence, aren't the "Nos" just a predictable metric result that you *must* have alongside of the "Yes" to make the numbers prove out? If we take the gross commission you'll receive for the "Yes" (let's say $1,500), and divide it by five, each "No" represents $300 in your pocket.

Pros have a very definite mind-set on this. Everything is reframed as an unemotional metric result. They drive their prospects to a definite result as quickly as they can. They carefully analyze their results and the data to ensure that their conversion ratios are sound. Then, they do one more thing; they sit back and smile each day, because "Yes" or "No," they know they are getting paid!

I'll finish up this Pipeline chapter by sharing with you a lesson I was taught by a person I met when I was in the business of multilevel marketing. If you know anything about MLM, then you know it's more about recruiting people to sell for you (building a downline organization) than just selling products yourself. Hence, the sale you're usually trying to make is to a person or a married couple, and you're trying to persuade them to start a home-based business. Needless to say, it's a rather tough sale, and there is a ton of rejection.

One night, after a recruitment meeting, I was downcast. I was only twenty-one years old at the time and was trying to build the business part-time while also continuing to sell insurance. I'd had a couple of no-shows that night, and the only guy that did show up laughed at me. There was an older man at the meeting, probably just over sixty. His name was Stan.

Stan approached me and asked if I was "okay." I told him I wasn't and went on to tell him that I was questioning if I were "cut out" to build an MLM business. He listened carefully and then offered me some sage advice. It is a piece of guidance that I treasure to this day.

"Ya know young man, if you're trying to do something different in this world, like trying to sell people on a concept that they don't fully understand, there's gonna' be folks that are not open-minded. Some people are gonna' be just plain mean."

Then he opened up his folio and wrote some letters on his yellow pad.

"It seems to me that your job isn't to worry about all of that nonsense. The way another person reacts, or thinks, is out of your control. Your job is to keep telling your story over and over again with a smile on your face. Your job is to keep your calendar full. You don't really know who's going to bite."

He ripped the yellow note page he'd written on out of his folio and handed it to me.

"Take this," he firmly instructed. "Tattoo this on your forehead or tape it to your bathroom mirror. It will save you from a lot of worries about nothing."

The note page he handed me had seven big letters written on it:

SWSWSWN

"SOME WILL, SOME WON'T, SO WHAT—NEXT!" he stated emphatically.

He patted me on the back and walked away. I almost quit the business that night—was on my way out the door if he hadn't talked to me—but there's more to the story.

I went on to build one of the largest distributorships on the West Coast for that organization. During my five-year tenure, I learned more about people and business than most people learn in a lifetime. That business served as a catalyst that enabled me to make millions in future endeavors.

Some will, some won't, so what—*next!* Those are seven powerful words for you to internalize if you plan to make it in commission sales. One more thing—those seven words can fairly well describe exactly how you should manage your Pipeline!

PART V

Solving The Equation

CHAPTER 20

When You Keep Score

Your CAP Score© Improves

"If winning isn't everything, why do they keep score?"

—**VINCE LOMBARDI,** legendary NFL player and coach

We've spent the first four parts of this book preparing you for, and teaching you the three key components of The CAP Equation©. This last section of the book will help you put everything together and explore the last few pieces of the puzzle. In this chapter, we will talk about where you are at now—help you honestly assess what your level of knowledge or ability is on each of the three main components of The CAP Equation©. You will assign yourself a CAP Score©.

I want to stress that you don't have to be highly skilled—an expert, at any of the components or sub elements we've identified. Becoming an expert at any or all of these areas might take months or years. If you're following the conceptual track of this book, you know that you don't have years to learn before you begin to earn. You must survive, and you survive because you are completing and solving the equation, putting all three components into play.

You won't survive if you get stuck on one of the pieces. If you're trapped—trying to become an expert at one or more of any of the elements we have discussed—versus simply moving to an adequate capability, you will stall out.

Allow me to paint a picture of what it looks like when a person becomes hopelessly stuck on perfection—or becomes addicted to education—and doesn't dive into the game of *execution*. I've been a competitive golfer since age thirteen, and I tend to relate a lot of what I've learned from tournament golf to my sales and entrepreneurial worlds.

I want to describe a type of golfer we like to poke gentle fun at. He's a person we call "Ranger Rick." This is the satirical name tied to the type of golfer who already has a good swing but still spends a lot of time on the practice range working on it—trying to perfect it. Ranger Rick invests hours on the range beating large buckets of striped practice balls. Ranger Rick takes lessons, and has analysts video his swing. He spends gobs of money on the latest equipment.

Don't get me wrong; these practices aren't necessarily bad. It's good to practice your skills; it's great to seek coaching; and it's a good idea to have the best tools. The problem comes when Ranger Rick gets stuck there on the practice range and doesn't get *into* the game. You see, Ranger Rick doesn't really *play* golf. He doesn't spend time in the heat of battle. He's perpetually stuck in the process of perfection. In Ranger Rick's mind, he has to be close to perfect at every facet of the game before he can tee it up in competition, but he never gets into the game. Rick is too busy seeking perfection to take his game to the course and perform, but he has a nice set of golf sweaters in his closet.

I have experienced the pain of watching many a professional student fail at commission sales. The pattern is identifiable. They say things like, "I'm not ready to go into the field and make a presentation," or, "I need to spend more time on my scripting. I'm still tripping over a few words." Hogwash! Simply become a 3 on our scale (adequate capability), and then let's go. The fastest way to go from 3 to 5 is by *doing*, not sitting in a classroom.

Don't be a Ranger Rick! Become comfortable with developing your Competencies, Attitudes and Pipeline practices to a 3 and then launch—get in the game. *Stumble* forward.

Assuming you have built a complete list of Competencies, Attitudes and Pipeline practices then let's go over the rating system and make sure you know where you are and what action(s) you need to take.

SAMPLE RATINGS FOR COMPONENTS

Level 1—No Level of Understanding

An honest rating of 1 simply means you have no knowledge of this particular element. It most likely indicates that you are brand-spanking new to sales, and I also assume that you have not attended any company-sponsored training sessions up to this juncture. In a rare case, your organization might not have training on this proficiency. Whatever the case, *your* job is to *find* the resources and get to a 3 as quickly as possible. You need to be in the game, and you can't take a 1 into battle.

Level 2—Limited Knowledge

If you rate yourself a 2 at any given skill or mindset, it might mean that you have carried over some limited amount of knowledge from another gig. It could also be that you are in the middle of training and still unsure of your proficiency. It might be that you are done with the company-sponsored training and something didn't stick. Regardless of the reason you are a 2, you must immediately determine what part of the skill set you're missing or unsure of and yell for *help*. My suggestion is for you to schedule time with your direct manager to drill and rehearse, or gain the information needed to get to a 3. Bottom line—you can't take proficiency levels of 1 or 2 into the field and expect to have good results.

Level 3—Adequate Capability

Bingo! This is what we call *good enough*. If you are a 3, it means that you can function at the given task with enough of a skill level to enable you to "stumble forward." Your job in the area of competencies is to grind on your list of core skills until they all rate a 3. When that happens, you can jump into the game and get some wins.

Level 4—Strong Abilities

As you take your level-3 proficiencies out onto the field of play, they will naturally improve to a level 4. In fact, they will improve much faster when practiced in the heat of battle. You will have genuine and real-time feedback as to how effective you are—or are *not*—at any given competency. The market will give you perfectly unfiltered feedback, if you are listening.

Don't overcorrect when the feedback and results come your way. Simply get with your trainer and make the gentle corrections necessary to improve your results. Above all else, don't use primetime to make corrections. Remember, only fine-tuning is needed at this point. Work on going from a 3 to a 4 or from a 4 to a 5 on your nonprime time.

Level 5—Highly Skilled

Congratulations! Go work on something else!

On the following page there is an image of the CAP Score© worksheet you will use to score your Competencies, Attitudes and Pipeline Practices. Please go to our website resource and download a complimentary copy of this form:

www.thecapequation.com/resources/

CAP SCORE Worksheet

Set Expectation(s) ➔ Access the resources to meet the Expectations ➔ Monitor your progress and seek Feedback ➔ Analyze results

Instructions: Please rate yourself in each category and provide notes to your coach prior to coaching session

Rating Key: Level 1 = No Competency / Level 2 = Limited Knowledge / Level 3 = Adequate Capability
Level 4 = Strong Ability / Level 5 = Highly Skilled

Competencies	1-5	+ Attitudes	1-5	× Pipeline	1-5
Core Competencies		**Attitudes/Thought Processes**		**Pipeline Mgmt. Practices**	
Industry Knowledge		Purpose/ Vision		New Leads Volume	
Target/Geo Market(s)		Faith/Confidence		Sustained Prospecting Flow	
Core Product Knowledge		Commitment/Determination		New Account Pipeline	
General Communication Skills		Coachability		Service Pipeline	
Unique Selling Proposition		Personal Responsibility		Using a CRM	
Raw Lead Generation		The Work		Pushing to "NO"	
New Appointment Generation		Risk		Conversion Ratios	
Presentation & Trial Closing		Sense of Urgency		Metric Result Practice	
Overcoming Objections/Stalls		Managing Expectations			
Facilitation/Enrollment		Failure/Rejection			
Asset Management		Emotional Controls			
Referral Generation System		Execution/Focus			
Time & Priority Management		Value of Time			
		Benchmarks			
		Humility			
PAR = 39		**PAR = 45**		**PAR = 24**	

Top 3 opportunities for improvement	*Top 3 opportunities for improvement*	*Top 3 opportunities for improvement*
#1	#1	#1
#2	#2	#2
#3	#3	#3

For more information. support and resources please ao to: www.CAPeauation.com/resources/

CHAPTER 21

Goal Seeking

Establishing Logical and Aligned Objectives

"If you can tune into your purpose and really align with it, setting goals so that your vision is an expression of that purpose, then life flows much more easily."

—JACK CANFIELD

If you give me your attention for just a few more chapters, I'll teach you a little bit about goal setting, how to properly use coaching, and how to successfully avoid distractions. Then we will be done with you, and you can put The CAP Equation© into motion for your career. This chapter is dedicated to some thoughts on goal setting.

It was January 2001. I was a state manager for a Fortune 500 insurance company. As was our custom, we were holding kickoff meetings at each of

the regional sales offices that I was responsible for. After the business an-
nouncements and training topics were completed, the regional sales manager asked each agent to walk up to the white board and sign in for his or
her annual sales goal. This was a public commitment to what they wanted
to achieve that year.

One by one, the agents and managers wrote their sacred promises
on the big board. Some of the numbers seemed a tad overstated to me,
and conversely, some appeared way too conservative. All the same, we
clapped for each person brave enough to come forward. I generally re-
served comment, that is, until one particular veteran agent went up to
the board to sign in.

We will call him Larry. Larry snatched the pen out of the regional manager's hand and signed in for $250,000. There was a resounding ovation
while his manager high-fived him. When Larry returned to his seat against
the back wall, next to me, I leaned over and asked him, "Hey, you've never
produced more than fifty-five grand in a year. That's a big number you put
up on the board, Larry...you got a few big cases on the horizon we don't
know about?"

He responded, "Nah. I don't have any big cases coming up. I don't guess
I'll do any more than I did last year."

I couldn't let his response drop there.

"Well, you did $45,000 last year," I commented. "Why did you just sign
in for $250,000?"

He looked at me with a twisted smile and answered, "Well, big sign-in
numbers make our manager so darn happy."

Larry was right. The regional manager of that office was ecstatic, but
the numbers he was feverishly adding up weren't going to occur, and there
certainly wasn't any accountability to the goal-setting process in that office. After that meeting, I thought long and hard about how we were setting goals as a team and individually. It was then that I began to ask people
to establish and communicate their goals differently.

I began to challenge our managers first, and then our agents, to resist
the hype and pressure, feeling they had to sign in with humongous num-

bers. Although I knew there was some magic in the practice of having someone write a swollen sales projection on the board, I also knew that if the number wasn't believable to them, it would be as if they had never made a commitment at all.

In other words, if a salesperson couldn't imagine doing more than $100,000 of production, but under peer pressure, committed to $250,000, the salesperson might as well have taken a pass on the exercise and simply said, "I'll do the amount of production I stumble into, so please leave me alone...and here's your stupid Magic Marker back!"

First and foremost, you must personally believe in your goals. They have to be numbers that are achievable in your mind. However, we, as leaders, don't ever want to sabotage the concept of thinking big. Getting salespeople to stretch their minds and dream big is a key factor in getting them to break out. We wish to honor both sides of the concept. Our objective is to incorporate reasonable thinking with some crazy dream building. To accomplish this, a few of us created a goal-setting and reporting method we called M-T-S. M-T-S stands for:

MINIMUM–TARGET–STRETCH

This is a very simple concept. Let's say you want to set a production goal for your first year. You will first establish a *minimum* goal or objective.

YOUR MINIMUM GOAL

This is the least amount of production necessary in order for you to survive in your sales position, pay your regular expenses, and satisfy your self-employment tax responsibility. You should backtrack to determine the production number needed. For purposes of this example, let's say that the number is $150,000 of sales production.

YOUR TARGET GOAL

This is the production number you'd *ideally* like to hit. It would allow you to do all of the above and also put some money in savings so that you can work toward a down payment on a home or fund your IRA. This projection benchmark would be a very comfortable place for you to be after year one. Let's say the number is $200,000.

YOUR STRETCH GOAL

This goal is where you get to have some fun. You get to *dream*, get a little crazy! What we want you to do here is throw out a production number that makes you giggle. This number may allow you to slap that down payment on a home or condo by year's end, no questions asked. It might allow you to upgrade your vehicle or pay off student loans. It isn't a number you can easily see yourself doing. Let's say the number is $300,000. Write this *crazy, unbelievable* goal down. This is the number we are actually going to do something with!

"Whoa", you say. "This $300,000 production number is two times my minimum goal...but, you said, 'You have to personally believe in your goals,'" Joe. "You said they have to be numbers you know you can do. They have to be achievable in your mind."

Yeah...I know I said that, but here's what the pros do...

They first establish a *minimum, take it to the bank* goal. This is a number they know they can achieve. Then, they extend that number to a more fulfilling projection, one that is still attainable but is a *target* goal. Then, they get all crazy and ask what the sales record is. That number becomes their *stretch* goal. This is the number they plan their *activity* around!

The pros have minimum and target goals. They are very reasonable and attainable, but all they fixate on is their *stretch* goals. Their stretch goals are exciting! They incite the passion they need to get out of bed each morning. It's the number that drives them!

Do they always hit those stretch goals? No. In most cases, they fall short, and they are either in-between minimum and target or target and stretch. But, they usually blow away the minimum goals because they built all of their activities around their *stretch* goals.

Is this making sense to you? I hope so. If you are new to sales and you establish one number, one goal (usually a minimum projection), and you fixate on it, build your activity around it—heaven help you. You might get lucky and hit it, but more often, you will fail to reach it. Think about it—if your minimum goal is $150,000, and you carefully build your activities to hit that number, you will have to be spot on with everything you do to hit it. There is no margin for error! Kind of dumb, don't you think?

Many of the 20% structure and set three levels of goals and they build all their efforts and activities around their *stretch* goals. Then, if they fail, they are still way ahead of any of their minimum income needs.

Let's talk about the elements that make up a logical set of goals and objectives. Allow me to offer you a formula that includes all of the vital factors that make up smart goals.

QUACK

A good part of my professional career was spent coaching and training salespeople and sales leaders for Aflac. You might recognize this great company for their iconic spokesperson—or should I say, "spokes-duck." As an acknowledgment to the great work we did there I want to offer you this memorable goal setting formula and acronym:

Q – Quantifiable
U – Understandable
A – Achievable
C – Controllable
K – Known

That's right; before you run around quacking out some half-baked goals, we're going to ask you to formulate them based on this effective blueprint.

Quantifiable

Your goals and objectives in every area have to be *measurable*. The goal has to have a defined outcome. If your goals are not measurable, then seek counsel from the person who's coaching you.

Understandable

I like *simple*. If your goals are *not clear*, you are handicapped from the start. Seek to have goals that are as close to concrete as possible. If you're assigned any goals or objectives that you don't understand, please seek counsel.

Achievable

We've shown you the M-T-S method. While your stretch goal might not be completely realistic in your own mind (initially), we will use it to build and drive your activities around. The balance of your goals *must be* realistic. Your objectives must be within your ability to complete them successfully. If they're not, please seek counsel with the person who is mentoring you.

Controllable

I'm not a big fan of any goal or objective that *depends* on somebody else. If your goals require help, then you had better make sure you figure out how to gain the competencies or resources you'll need to perform the tasks on your own. I am also not a fan of any goal that you can't start working toward immediately—*today*.

Known

Are your goals known? Who have you *shared* them with? We are obviously suggesting that you seek out an "accountability partner." I will also challenge you to write your goals down and tape them to your refrigerator, bathroom mirror, or wherever you will see them several times each day.

Look, it's easy to establish benchmarks and then get a little bit off track, get down on yourself, and then give up on them. We've all been there. It's much harder to give up on your goals if others know about them. The best person to share them with is your sales coach or mentor.

If you're so inclined, you might also want to share your objectives with your spouse or significant other. They have some skin in the game, a vested interest in your success. They will help motivate you when the going gets tough.

This is the QUACK method of setting your goals. These are the parameters I use when establishing objectives for my business as well as my personal life. This template will help you clarify what your goal should look like and help you reach it.

ADDITIONAL FINANCIAL GOALS TO CONSIDER

There are two other important pieces of information I'd like to share with you that pertain to your financial obligations and your financial future.

Tax-Planning Goals

There is a prevalent mishandling of this issue by self-employed salespeople, and I've found that a little planning and forethought can go a long way. If you are truly commission-only (1099), then you will receive a gross commission check from the organization you work with. It will not have any state or federal taxes (or other statutory obligations) withheld from it. Hence, from day one, you must plan to set aside the monies needed to satisfy those issues. This means that before you establish income goals that satisfy your personal obligations, that goal must also take taxes and self-employment issues into consideration. Your net income, after your estimated tax obligations are calculated, should be what you live on, not your gross commission checks.

The employer you're receiving commission from should issue you a 1099 after the tax year is over. It will reflect the gross commission income they paid you. This is the figure that you will have to declare to the IRS. Certain allowable business expenses can be deducted from that gross income on an itemized basis (usually filed on a Schedule C). I'm certainly not qualified to offer tax advice. You would be wise to connect with a reputable Certified Public Accountant who is familiar with self-employment issues and tax laws.

Retirement-Planning Goals

There is one other financial item you should consider budgeting for if you are self-employed. Generally, you won't have access to a 401(k), pension plan, or retirement vehicle sponsored by an actual employer. My suggestion would be that you seek out a retirement professional who specializes in advising self-employed people. You might choose to establish a self-directed pension plan. There are a myriad of tax laws and formulas that can be used, as well as some very good investment vehicles.

In many cases, your CPA will be able to refer you to an investment advisor as well as a pension actuary to set this up for you. Even if you can only set aside a few thousand dollars a year, it is my strong suggestion to begin a plan like this.

One last note on this subject: I have seen some very talented salespeople do everything else right, except handle their tax and retirement obligations. It's not a pretty picture if you get down the road and have neglected these important obligations. You surely don't want to perish at the hands of your own negligence—or worse, at the hands of the IRS!

The key points I'd like you to take away from this chapter are that you should be thoughtful about your actual goals and the processes you use to establish them. Too many new salespeople fail to choose goals that will support their income needs, and some of those goals are far too nebulous to attain or manage.

Now you know how the pros establish their goals and the factors that comprise them. No excuses. Set your goals wisely and thoughtfully.

CHAPTER 22

Check-Up from the Neck-Up

How to Use Coaches

"Whatever you do in life, surround yourself with smart people who'll argue with you."

—JOHN WOODEN

This might be the most essential chapter in the book if you have a tendency to dream big but aren't the most accountable person in the room. I have personally traveled in and out of the realm of being coachable and accountable throughout my long career. I can assure you that in my most lucrative years, I was very open to being mentored and most eager to have a coach. Flying solo was never the best bet for me.

179

I'm going to break this subject up into two silos—two types of coaching and mentoring that I have successfully used over the years. I will refer to these two types of counsel as *internal* and *external coaching*. By *internal coaching*, I mean any direction or counsel you may receive or access *inside* of the organization or company you sell for. *External coaching* will refer to any and all mentoring you gather *outside* of the organization you are a part of. Both internal and external coaching is critical and serves to offer you different benefits. Let's look at internal coaching first.

INTERNAL COACHING

The organization or company you sell products or programs for should want to coach you and instruct you like your life depends on it—because it does. In my experience, some are more fervent in this area than others; however, if your organization doesn't have a proactive stance on this, you should force the issue.

There are critical benchmarks early in every sales career when you have to stop, ask some key questions, and assess your progress. You have to get real and perform what I refer to as a "check-up from the neck-up." The type of checkup we are referring to in this chapter is a deep dive; a counseling session that serves as a review of your current Competencies, Attitudes, Pipeline, calendar management, goals, even some personal issues if they're relevant to your survival.

I strongly suggest that you hard-wire (schedule) several deep-dive checkups with your direct manager (primary sales trainer or coach) after 30, 60, 90, and 180 days. The most critical of the four timelines listed above are the 90-day and the 180-day checkups.

The reason those two benchmarks in time are so critical is that, based on my experience, I have rarely seen salespeople who are on target at 90 days *not* make it through their first year successfully. Conversely, when salespeople are well *off target* at 90 days, I've rarely seen them become successful unless they significantly altered their course.

The 90-day mark is the time for salespeople and their coaches to assess what is going *right*, celebrate those things, and make small corrections or tweaks if necessary. What if things are going *wrong*? It is the time for them to huddle up with their coaches and inspect each and every facet of their game. It is the time to make vital corrections quickly.

The 180-day mark also has significance. I discovered early in my sales-management career that it doesn't take a year or even nine months to know if a salesperson is going to make it in sales. A person should know by the six-month mark whether or not he or she is going to make it in commission sales. I've rarely been wrong on this one. If a commission salesperson is crashing and burning at six months, it rarely, if ever, gets any better. By the 180-day mark, people should know, in their heart, if they need to stay or move on. Of course, they will come to this conclusion as long as they're not deceiving themselves.

If their internal sales coaches are doing their jobs, they're also making the proper recommendations. There are some organizational cultures that will try to keep a salesperson around as long as they can regardless of the toll it is taking on the person, family, or finances. Reputable sales managers will tell you like it is.

I will revert back to the earlier lessons in this book and suggest that this isn't rocket science. If you are not cutting it at the 90-day or 180-day mark, it's because you have failed to employ the principles of The CAP Equation© in its entirety. In other words, if you really understand the subject matter in this book, you could probably coach yourself and ask the key questions.

I am now going to break down for you what you need to be looking for at each of the timelines I have suggested.

30-Day Check-Up

Perform a hard evaluation of your core Competencies, keying in on the following:

- Your knowledge of the market and your core products/programs
- Presentation and closing skills
- Your lead supply and your Pipeline-management practices
- Your calendar and time-management issues

If you are *not* completely wired on any of the above Competencies, immediately draft a plan with your coach to become so within the next seven to ten business days! Competency in these areas is vital, and time is of the essence. In addition, and so you don't miss anything, ask yourself the following questions:

- How is my confidence level?
- What books am I reading?
- Have I established achievable, short-term goals?
- Do I have an accountability partner? (At work and at home)
- Is my calendar full? (Enough so to support my stated goals)
- Am I continuing to add new raw leads to my Pipeline?
- Am I driving prospects to a definite result? ("Yes" or "No")
- Have I asked my coach what he or she is concerned about?
- What am I most concerned about?
- What is my definite checklist of action items?
- What do I need to complete before the 60-day checkup?

A 30-day review should conclude with a solid list of action points to be worked on or completed prior to the next scheduled coaching session.

60-Day Check-Up

A 60-day coaching session with your direct manager and perhaps with a manager from a higher level should be held to review your progress since the 30-day mark. It should encompass many of the same questions listed above and include a hard look at those areas that were marked for improvement. This should be the time that both parties agree that activities and skill sets are trending or improving at a rate that will support a successful quarter of production. If not, then immediate steps should be taken to alter your course.

90-Day Check-Up

This is that critical point in time I previously described, kind of a telling benchmark. At 90 days, you should schedule a coaching session with your direct manager and senior management to determine your overall growth and development patterns. This should be a two-way conversation that addresses their satisfaction level with your performance as well as yours. There are a few piercing questions that you should ask at this benchmark:

- Am I making a living—covering my expenses?
- If not—why not?
- What are the specific challenges? (Can I quantify them?)
- How can I correct the challenges in a short time curve?
- Do I have enough reserves to stay in the game?

If your activities and results are trending nicely, then no worries! You'll get a pat on the back from your manager, and you're off to keep loading new leads into your Pipeline and close a few more of them. However, if you're crashing and burning, it's time to huddle together with your manager and *fix some things that are broken, and fix them fast!*

180-Day Check-Up

This should be a clear moment of truth for you and your internal coach. You are either making it or you're *not* at the six-month mark. From the perspective of over thirty-five years of experience, if you are failing miserably at this stage, no additional time, training, or coaching is going to make much of a difference unless you are literally in a financial or emotional position to start over.

At the 90-day mark, you are looking to correct your path if you are off target. If you draft a definite plan for improvement and stick to it over the subsequent 180 days, you should be fine. If after another three months of hard work and correction, you're not back on target, you have to ask much tougher questions of yourself and the organization you're with:

- Am I saying the right things? (Do I know how to present?)
- Am I confident in my entire set of core Competencies?
- Are my activity levels commensurate with my income goals?
- Are the numbers working the way they said they would?
- Is my company's product competitive?

- Is there a problem in my industry? (Market/economic factors)
- Am I being coached properly? (Adequate upline support)

And the final (and most important) question you should ask is...

- Do I *like* this work? Do I have a passion for this?

The last question is critical. If what you are selling, the company you represent, and the people you work with don't supply you with energy, you aren't going to be able to keep pushing through the wall. If you don't have a *passion* for the work you're doing after six months, it's time for you to check out. You'd be wise to go find some other gig!

One last thought on your first six months and the internal coaching you receive: If you're hard-headed and think a little more time on the job would make a difference, then give yourself only one more month, but work that month like your life depends on it—because at least your financial life *does* depend on it!

EXTERNAL COACHING

I am asked this type of question all the time. It always comes out sounding something like this:

> "Joe, I'm starting to do good in my role, but I think I can do better. My manager is great, but she's really busy. Should I seek additional professional sales coaching outside of my organization?"

If salespeople aren't outright asking this question, I can assure you that they are at least wondering if they would benefit financially from external coaching and mentoring. This thought surfaces because you are probably being prodded daily to produce more, and your manager is also admonishing you to become better at your job.

Think about it, most sales managers encourage you to become more skilled at prospecting, presenting, closing, and so on. They'll tell you that you need to sharpen up your game, yet, if you investigate, you'll find less skill-set coaching is occurring inside an organization than might be expected, given management's ranting. Why is that? While there are a multitude of places you could lay blame, here are a few of the more common reasons.

Contrasting Agendas

Your direct sales manager can and should be a key source of great coaching for you. Unfortunately, they get bogged down in the whirlwind of administrative tasks. They want to coach and train you, but it gets put off till Wednesday, then Friday, and then...it never happens.

You Become a Victim of Your Great Production

Last month's numbers were tabulated and they look good. So, the motivation to offer you more training and coaching tends to wane. If it's not broken, then why try to fix it, right?

Zombie Home-Office Apocalypse

Sometimes, inadequate or flawed training platforms from the home office in Keokuk, Iowa just won't die. The training program developed in 1984 keeps coming back to life, and you have to learn it and nothing else. "We've already put in place a great sales-training curriculum; additional internal coaching is not considered a real necessity. Go do your job."

Shiny New Objects

New, unproven training programs can sometimes seduce sales leadership. They might believe that these new ideas, alone, will save or resurrect sales production. They become distracted by the theoretical concept in front of them and lose sight of the global approach to training. They may have a tendency to lose their commitment to personal coaching efforts.

Bottom line—internal coaching doesn't happen in a pervasive fashion without consistent and conscious leadership support, and too often that support is compromised by all of the factors above and more causes that we did not list. For these reasons, if you want to get better at what you do, join the 20 percent, and realize your income potential, you will need to seek external coaching and mentoring.

If you're a lone-wolf salesperson who thinks you can *go it alone,* I'd like to offer you some thoughts on this subject. I was in that mind-set more than once over my long career, but would always become open again to coaching or mentoring when I inevitably lost my way. It was at those times that I turned to additional coaching and, subsequently, began to grow again. I will be eternally grateful to the mentors who hung in there with me.

If you're struggling with accepting help, let me summarize with five points what the right coach will do for you.

1. *Clarity*

The right sales or leadership coach will help you define your objectives and help you tap into your energy so that you can properly focus and engage.

2. *Execution*

A good coach will assist you in the execution process, helping you to develop the right habits. Developing and altering habits can feel like a root canal; however, a regular meeting with the right mentor helps you become hyperaware of your bad habits so that you can minimize them. The more you know your behavior is being observed, the more likely you will be to stay on course.

3. *Guidance*

Sales mentors can guide you—ask you probing questions so that you can find your own answers. They can also offer direct advice about specific actions or results they observe.

4. *Skill-set Development*

The right coach will assess your skills, knowledge, and attribute development. Growth-related gaps often become obvious when there is an honest two-way dialogue. Coaches can recommend additional training so that you can convert a weakness into a strength.

5. *Motivation*

Sales mentors will understand the underlying motivators of each individual they coach and take action to maximize them.

We are not meant to handle this difficult growth process alone. If we allow a coach or mentor to engage with us, and if we share our faults honestly with them, a truly synergistic and collaborative environment will flourish.

If you want to know more about what a sound coaching process (group or personal) looks like, please visit our website:

www.thecapequation.com/coaching/

CHAPTER 23

Invisible Noise

A Whirlwind of Distractions

"One way to boost our willpower and focus is to manage our distractions instead of letting them manage us."

—**DANIEL GOLEMAN,** psychologist, author

I want to dedicate this last chapter to a nebulous but hazardous issue. It's an imperceptible monster that can sabotage all of your hard work in developing Competencies, Attitudes, and Pipeline practices. It can swallow up the smartest and most talented people and spit them out. I call this prodigious disruptor *invisible noise.*

Why do seemingly talented salespeople still sometimes fail to achieve their personal goals or even survive in sales? *Often the answer lies in their inability to block out distractions and focus on the priorities.* The truth is, eager salespeople can soak in and apply everything that is written in this book and still *fail* if they allow the *invisible noise* to encroach into their prime time.

In this chapter, we discuss "invisible noise"—the unsolicited and often haphazard interference injected into an otherwise well-planned workday. There are three common forms of invisible noise. You will need to identify and manage each kind if you're planning to survive and thrive. All forms of interference are mostly unsolicited. They can best be categorized as *digital distractions, human distractions, and paper distractions*. Let's discuss the digital sort of interference first.

DIGITAL DISTRACTIONS

These can find you on many platforms and be thrust on you by total strangers or your closest confidants. I'll describe the habits of a few friends of mine. They happen to be very smart, driven, and successful people; however, they are easily distracted. At any given time, even if I am trying to have a face-to-face conversation with them, they'll have Facebook or Twitter open on their mobile devices. They'll be checking e-mails, responding to texts, or have multiple IM conversations going. What's worse, I've also witnessed them and others trying to perform all of these digital tasks while prospecting or following up with clients.

These digital distractions now find us 24/7. It's way too easy to become bombarded with communication in today's transparent world. It's as if we have a GPS device duct taped to our right hand. Everyone knows how to reach us all the time. Information (important or not), messages (critical or not), and memos (urgent or not), seem to fly at us at warp speed. Worse, those on the other end sometimes expect an immediate response. If you are in commission sales, your job is to be face-to-face with a prospect, not wading through a swamp of digital minutia. You can't possibly focus on prospecting or selling if you allow yourself to be constantly *distracted*.

The truth is, the bulk of all digital communication isn't important or urgent. Think of it this way—a lot of what's being delivered to your desktop or mobile device is the equivalent of electronic banana peels, trying to trip you up. To assist you with this challenge, we're going to supply you with a "digital communication rule" that will help you proactively manage these distractions.

Digital Communication Rule

Only check your incoming electronic messages *four times* per day. *Limit* yourself to 15-20 minute sessions of retrieval and response. Below is a schedule that I try to adhere to:

1. 7:30 a.m.–Before your first sales calls
2. 11:45 a.m.–Before or during lunch
3. 4:00 p.m.–Near the end of your workday
4. 6:00 p.m.–After your workday is over, but not during family time

Other than the times listed above, you should turn your mobile device *off*, or at least switch it to "silent" and put it out of sight. The logic in this practice is that if you schedule very specific times to check and clear your communications, you'll only spend an hour of concentrated time (4×15 minutes) on this task, versus squandering two hours or more of your precious day; conversely, the time that you have demarcated in your calendar for prospecting, selling, or whatever you have deemed a priority will be better-focused time, yielding superior results.

Think about this very simple digital communication rule and what it can achieve for you. If you add up the potentially squandered digital communication time (two hours per day multiplied by five workdays), it equals ten hours per week. Based on a four-week month, that equals a total of forty hours. That means—by *not* having a firm digital communication rule—you might be wasting an *entire week* each month! You are losing one week per month of prime selling time simply so that you can read unsolicited spam on your mobile device or post a comment on Facebook about your friend's pet poodle that's wearing a small cowboy hat.

HUMAN DISTRACTIONS

Sometimes, what you *don't* do is just as important as what you *do* decide to do. I loved the segment called "Stupid Human Tricks" on the *Late Show with David Letterman*, but stupid human tricks are my least favorite thing in commission sales. Human distractions can come at you from two directions in the workplace: your hierarchy or your peers. Let's break down and discuss both types. We will refer to those driven by your hierarchy as "The Sales Prevention Department." Those distractions caused by your coworkers will be referred to as "Peer Parasites."

The Sales Prevention Department

When you begin your sales career, what you really need from your hierarchy is helpful support. Then, once you're off and running, you want them to stay out of your way; however, it doesn't always work that way. "The Sales Prevention Department" is anyone in your hierarchy that wants you to engage in any activity that takes you away from productivity. It can be a well-meaning person, even your direct manager.

Corporate America—and many other 1099 organizations—are riddled with examples of how sales management can trip over their own two feet. Somebody can have a great idea for a new type of *magic bullet* presentation that can increase closing averages. Or the new Sr. V.P. who just came into the ranks has a new training requirement that pulls people out of the field whether they're having success or not. It would all be comical if it weren't so distracting and costly. This kind of nonsense goes on a lot in the sales game.

As you get past your first 180 days, you'll need to be cognizant of these organizational dynamics and begin to raise your guard. Let's take a look at some of the sales deterrents that might be thrown in your path by your hierarchy. Let's also discuss suggestions for avoiding them or at least limiting their negative impact on your growth.

Sales Meetings

I could write a book on the topic of sales meetings gone bad; however, for the sake of staying on course, let me simply suggest that you need to be aware of what the actual value is of any sales meeting you're asked to attend. My experience tells me that if you are reporting to a manager who has solid leadership skills and one who puts thought and effort into meetings, then that manager might be of great value to you, especially when you are quite new and need to feel a part of something.

However, the reverse can also be true. The periodic meetings might be poorly planned and merely a vanity vehicle for the manager holding them. In other words, the meetings make the manager feel in control, but they don't add real value to your career. If the meetings run long, then they could be robbing you of prime selling or family time. If you are a W2 employee and compelled to attend these meetings, then you must attend them. If you are an independent contractor (1099), you might want to limit your time in them or cleverly avoid them altogether.

Ineffective Training Platforms

The typical scenario looks like this: someone in your hierarchy has decided that organizational sales can be increased through additional or ongoing classroom training. It could be an internal program or a series that came from an external vendor. Outside of new products being launched (and technical or compliance training), you should carefully evaluate these time-consuming programs and determine if you want to or need to commit buckets of time to them. Again, I'm assuming you are 1099 and you have a choice.

All too often these types of training programs are not organic. They aren't driven by the 20 percent, the top producers; they are driven top-down—someone's bright idea at the home office or worse—one designed by an outside consultant. Be very wary of these potential time killers.

Untested Projects/Markets

Red flares! You'll be cruising along, doing all the right things, making sales, and then, your sales manager will select you to pilot a new program, new market, or new product. If the new program is the least bit untested, then you might want to resist the urge to jump in with all fours. Proceed carefully. Don't be a guinea pig for someone else's new idea.

Management Training Programs

There might be a time for you to consider stepping into a formal management-training program for your company or organization. However, based on my experience, it's never prudent to consider one during the first six months, and rarely should one be considered before you have a successful first year under your belt. This can be a huge distraction to your successful sales career and your commission flow. Consider advancement, but be thoughtful about the timing and what role you are truly well suited for.

Mandatory/Optional CRM Tools (or any time-consuming software)

Many organizations have migrated to enterprise versions of CRMs (Customer Relationship Management Software) to track their leads and clients. They've also shifted toward asking their salespeople to adopt these platforms as well. In many cases, an independent salesperson will have to pay for these subscriptions and also invest time to learn how to use them. While I find many of these programs useful as you build up a large volume of data, I've also seen the adoption of a bulky CRM throw certain salespeople off course.

Be aware of what you are trying to accomplish with a CRM or any other complex software program. Make certain that someone demonstrates that it is the right tool for the job you're trying to accomplish before you commit your time and your money to it.

There are probably a few more potential distractions that can spring from "The Sales Prevention Department," but we will leave it here and simply warn you that you'll need to manage your managers. Nobody, including your manager, is going to respect your time and your space if you don't respect it first. Let's move on to the other kind of human distraction.

Peer Parasites

These other human distracters can best be described as well- meaning but disoriented bloodsuckers. These pests might loiter around your cubicle, waiting for an opportunity to socialize with you, or they can take the shape of *that guy* who follows you out to your car. They will try to lure you into "a cup of coffee at Starbucks" or whatever unproductive activity they've dreamed up for their Monday afternoons. These peer parasites are to be avoided at all costs.

You will also want to be cognizant of the messy political atmosphere that can exist in any organizational culture. Most sales units have definite factions—some positive, some negative. Some cliques are allied with management, and some are not. Early on, you'll have no idea which is which and what affect those relationships can have on your career.

The best thing to do when you are relatively new is to *not* align with any clique. After you've got at least six months under your belt, you'll be better able to identify the most positive and professional tribe. Stay neutral early on, be cognizant of the peer parasites, and only align yourself with those who are positive, professional, and can assist you in moving your career forward.

PAPER DISTRACTIONS

The third, most common type of distraction is that of paper or any other physical object that can land on your desk. The cultural thinking was that businesses would be paperless by this time in the digital age, but apparently my desk hasn't gotten that message yet. I have a very straightforward formula that you can use as a life raft for your sinking desk. Let's take a look at it.

The RAFT Formula (Route-Action-File-Trash)

The RAFT acronym will hopefully train your brain to place each piece of hard copy communication in one of four definite *categories* as soon as it hits your desk. The category will guide you in its disposition. This method is time-saving and will give you an efficient way of keeping your desk afloat with productive issues.

Route

Use this when the communication or issue needs to be reviewed, handled, or approved by someone else. Get the communication *off* your desk or desktop by routing it to the appropriate person. If it is paper and can be scanned (and doesn't need to be saved in hard copy), then scan it, e-mail it, and throw the hard copy away (or shred if applicable).

Action

This type of communication requires some attention by you. You should note the action and schedule the appropriate time to take the action that is required of you.

File (Paper or Digital)

This is when the communication must be saved in some format. If it can be protected in digital format, then scan it and file it in a digital folder, disposing of the hard copy. If the hard copy (original) needs to be kept, then create a physical file. Always remember: if the piece of paper you are holding contains information that can be easily accessed digitally, then you should not save that piece of paper. The key strategy is to get the communication out of your inbox or off your desk.

Trash

Dispose of any piece of communication that you do not need. If the information can be found through a quick Google search, then *trash* it. If it is junk or spam, then unsubscribe from the sender.

Hopefully, you can employ the RAFT method to solve your paper challenges and use some of the other concepts to lessen your digital and human distractions. I want to wrap up this chapter on "Invisible Noise" by addressing one other issue—something we have all been told we can do.

THE MULTITASKING MYTH

Please allow me to bust the myth surrounding a thing we call "multi-tasking." We'd like to believe that multi-tasking works and that it was recently invented for us. We'd like to believe that we could use multiple forms of digital media at once, while at the same time checking e-mails, talking to a client, reviewing a report, and drinking our decaf latte. We'd also like to believe that we are awesome at this multi-tasking thing!

In one of the letters he wrote to his son in the 1740s, Lord Chesterfield offered the following advice:

> "There is time enough for everything in the course of the day, if you do but one thing at once, but there is not time enough in the year, if you will do two things at a time. This steady and un-dissipated attention to one object is a sure mark of a superior genius; as hurry, bustle, and agitation are the never-failing symptoms of a weak and frivolous mind."

In Lord Chesterfield's way of thinking, *focus* was not merely a useful way to structure one's time; it was a sign of intelligence. I am not sure he was a big fan of multitasking, which apparently existed, in some form, back then also. If you subscribe to Lord Chesterfield's philosophies, multitasking doesn't work and hasn't worked since about the 1740s.

It has also been proven that heavy multitaskers engage in even heavier multitasking because their habits lead to a reduced ability to *filter out* interference and distractions ("invisible noise"). Although it is not scientifically proven, some researchers believe that the part of our brains that processes deeper cognitive thought actually atrophies in this whole practice of multitasking. In plain English, when we multitask, we might actually be *dumbing* ourselves down.

If that isn't enough to make you think about this social and cultural habit, in 2005, the BBC reported on a research study—funded by Hewlett-Packard and conducted by the Institute of Psychiatry at the University of London— that found:

> "Workers distracted by e-mail, digital media, and unsolicited phone calls suffer a fall in IQ more than twice that found in marijuana smokers."

Therefore, the next time you see someone who appears to be stoned, incoherent, or not completely present, that individual might not be high on weed but just might have wasted the morning with a marathon session on Facebook, Twitter, Instagram, Vine, Tumblr, LinkedIn, answering Gmail, or looking at videos on YouTube. I'm certainly not suggesting that social media created the age-old problem of distractions, but it has greatly expanded upon it.

We're in a different place and time than when I began selling in 1979. It was easier then to be in the field for hours, staying totally focused. There were no mobile devices. I was an island unto myself while out in the field. When I was done with one door, I'd turn right and walk into another. There were no digital distractions waiting for me in my right hand.

As I have become more conscious of how and when I'm most productive, it convinced me that I'm at my very best when focused on only one task at a time. I know; you are great at multitasking. Good luck with that. As for me, I'm going with Lord Chesterfield's advice.

What you should take away from this chapter should be fairly clear. "Invisible Noise" is all around us, and it can take many shapes and colors, even subtle ones we don't easily recognize. The most prescient point is that none of us are immune to the danger that distractions represent, even if we are competent professionals. To ensure your success using the lessons you've learned thus far in this book, I wanted to make you aware of and give you some tools to manage this "Invisible Noise." Creating solid habits by using some of the formulas and rules we've suggested is one sure way to stay on target with your stated goals.

CONCLUSION

The Conundrum

Getting Out of Your Own Way

"You have brains in your head. You have feet in your shoes. You can steer yourself in any direction you choose. You're on your own, and you know what you know, and you are the guy who'll decide where to go."

—DR. SEUSS

Let's stop and take a deep breath. We are done with academic lessons. I have given you a complete understanding of The CAP Equation©, hopefully cementing in your mind the elements you'll have to address to ensure your unlimited success in sales.

I've told you what profile traits you'll need. We've looked at the odds of making it, and then I told you how to tip those odds in your favor by thinking and acting like the 20 percent. We've dug deep into the three vital pieces of The CAP Equation© and challenged you to learn and practice them. I have told you that when you add the first two components together and then multiply them by the third factor, it virtually ensures your success in commission sales. Like the chilidog-munching fighter pilot told me in 1980, "It's foolproof."

I have delivered on my promise by exposing, proving, and teaching the premise; however, we've even gone one step further. In the last few supplementary chapters, we have addressed the subtle landmines that could trip you up, even if you have a relatively high CAP Score©. We've overdelivered. You know how the secret sauce is made. You're now in possession of the knowledge that the 20 percent all have—how they think, what they do. Just having this knowledge will absolutely ensure your success, right? All of the readers of my book—100 percent of them—will immediately go forth and become wealthy, right?

You know the answer. Not likely.

There is a conundrum that people like me will always have to wrestle with, an enduring enigma that remains after the teaching is done. If this whole thing called sales is as simple as a mathematical equation, one we've already been given the answer to, then why do people still choose to fail? Why do so many take this open-book test and refuse to walk up to the chalkboard and solve their own problems?

If I could join the individual conversations going on in each of your heads, I could give you the specific and correct answer, one that would pertain to you. But I can't; I'm not clairvoyant. I'm simply a professional salesperson and an experienced sales leader and trainer; however, if I had to venture a guess as to what one last piece of advice would help you, I would tell you to decide to get out of your own way.

Yeah, I know, that advice sounds trite; but it's probably the right remedy to solve any lingering challenges you might create for yourself. There's probably a small self-image glitch, or tinge of fear lingering in your noggin, or a combination of both. You don't want to think about it or admit it, but it's probably there, and it can hold you back if you don't acknowledge it.

Oftentimes, the last piece of this puzzle we call sales success is about believing in yourself. It's about looking at that top producer and noting that he puts his pants on one leg at a time, just as you do. It may be as simple as recognizing that the superstar salesperson in your organization has to get up in the morning and beat back her doubts and fears just like you do. And, yes...I don't care who you're looking up to, thinking, "I can never be as good as him or her," just know they're all a mess, dealing with their own perceived shortcomings and insecurities, too.

Every time I start to question my abilities, or inabilities, I think back about my first week on the job with Penn Life, an eighteen-year-old, selling those $39 accident policies. I recall how frightened I was. Then I smile, knowing that within a few months I was able to find a rhythm and begin to make a nice living. After my first year, I became the youngest field trainer in their history. Within two years, I was one of the top-producing managers in the state of California. In retrospect, my fears were silly. All I had to do was decide to get out of my own way.

Whenever I'm uncertain about how to tackle a new venture or project that I know little about, I think back on another day, the day back in 1995 when Aflac management offered me the opportunity to establish and build their market in Los Angeles. I almost didn't accept the position because I was so unsure of my executive leadership skills. I'm glad I ignored some of the destructive voices in my head. I'm pleased that I decided to get out of my own way once again. Over the next fourteen years, we built one of the most profitable and legendary sales organizations Aflac has ever had.

I became wealthy as a result of being in commission sales and sales management and have leveraged my knowledge into other profitable ventures as well, but there could have been another ending to my happy little story. My path to wealth in sales could have easily gone in a different direction if a person I respected and loved hadn't challenged me. I want to share just one last story with you before we close out this book. It represents the greatest lesson I've ever learned about sales, but the man who bestowed the message wasn't even *in* sales.

Penn Life was my first real outside-commission-sales experience. I told you that I learned a great deal while with them. I certainly had a measure of success to build on and take to the next gig. What I didn't tell you was that I almost quit outside sales completely in my first month of being there.

It was on a Friday afternoon in the late summer of 1979. I'd pulled out of the field early. I had had a bad week. I'd made a few sales but experienced too many crushing defeats for my delicate psyche. As the "Nos" piled up on me like shovels of wet sand, I became call reluctant. The reason I went home early that day was that I couldn't get out of my car and walk into another business. I was paralyzed by my feelings. My emotional gas tank was empty.

I was living at home with my parents. My father, "Buzz," cruised into the driveway, getting home just about dinnertime. While dishing himself some of my mom's spaghetti and meatballs, he asked me how my week went. I was honest with him; I told him I pulled out of the field early. I remember the conversation in vivid detail.

"I think I'm gonna' go in on Monday and quit," I told him. "I don't think this thing works, and I'm not sure I'm cut out for commission sales."

He leaned back in his chair. I could tell by the look on his face that he wasn't thrilled with my decision.

"Okay, Sport. You can do anything you want. It's your life. Quit if you want," he said. "But, I've never quit anything just because I was failing. If you want to quit, you should go out and have a solid week first, figure some things out, then tell them you're quitting. That way you'll be leaving for the right reasons—because you don't like the work—not because you're failing at the work. You can leave with your head held high, a winner."

It was hard to argue with his logic, but I was a teenager, so I had to try.

"Dad, yeah, I hear what you're saying, but this sales thing is hard. It's all cold calling, and I'm getting beat up out there. I'm not sure their process even works."

He nodded his head like he understood, but I could tell he wasn't going to let me off the hook.

"You got home at what time today?" he asked.

"About 2:30 p.m.," I reluctantly answered.

'Well, that doesn't sound like a full day's work," he sniffed. "How many cold calls did they tell you to make each day—how many doors do they want you to walk into?"

"Sixty," I told him.

"How many did you walk into today?" he asked.

I reached into my pocket and pulled out a small white card that Penn Life called "Countdown to Success." It had five columns for the five work-days and the numbers 1–60 printed vertically down each column.

You were supposed to cross out each number when you walked in the door and made an approach. You were to circle the numeral if a decision maker allowed you to give a presentation. You were then to place a number of units next to the circle if you sold something.

I glanced at my card. I noted there was no day that week that I'd walked into more than twenty doors, and my efforts had decreased daily as the week had worn on. There were a couple of circles each day and even a few sales. But when you were selling $39 accident policies, you had to have a lot of circles to make a living. That day represented my worst effort of the week. I'd only crossed off eight doors before getting back in my car and heading home with my tail between my legs.

"I walked into eight doors today," I finally admitted.

He leaned back again and rubbed his chin. I wasn't sure if he were going to unload on me or abide by my decision to quit sales. He was quiet for a moment; then he spoke.

"Ya know what I would do if I was you, Sport? I'd go out next week, walk into the sixty doors a day, each day, for the entire week, just like they taught you. Put their products and their system to the test. What's the worst that can happen...a few people kick you out? Win, lose, or draw, if you still don't like the work by the end of next week, you can quit. But you can walk away knowing you gave it your all. You can leave with your head held high, knowing you didn't cheat the system."

He went back to his dinner plate and didn't say anything else. The conversation was over. The ball was in my court. He was challenging me to set my emotions aside, put in a full workweek, and put the pressure on their system. I decided to follow his advice. I went out that next week with a slightly different attitude. I had only one clear objective, which was to cross out all sixty numbers on their "Countdown to Success" card each day so that I could prove it didn't work. I was obsessed with reaching that goal of walking into sixty doors each day. Without knowing it, when I was putting the pressure on the system, I was getting out of my own way.

By the close of business that Tuesday, I'd already sold twelve units—my best week ever. I'd begun to realize that if I walked into sixty doors each day, I didn't have to be a great salesperson or closer. Because I was focused on putting the pressure on the numbers, the rejection didn't seem to have any negative effect on me. I had removed my faulty emotions and fears from the equation. Buzz had challenged me to get out of my own way, and by doing so I'd stumbled onto one of the key concepts and attitudes that I would teach for the next thirty-five years. I reframed rejection into nothing more than a metric result versus a crushing emotional defeat.

I walked into at least sixty doors each day that week. On Thursday evening of that week, I stayed out until 7:45 p.m. trying to find the sixtieth person to approach. I had an awesome week! I sold thirty-two units and earned over $500 in commissions!

I was flying high and barely made it home in time for mom's dinner that next Friday night. My parents knew I was having a good week. I didn't have to tell them. My dad saw my energy and the smile on my face. The conversation that night with my dad was short and very sweet.

"So this was your last week?" Buzz asked. "You gonna' tell 'em you quit on Monday?"

He asked me that question knowing what my answer would be. I just smiled.

"Thanks for talking me off the cliff last week. Thanks for challenging me. I think I got the hang of this now."

And I did have the hang of it. I'd learned a valuable lesson, a lesson that was spurred on by my father's challenge and my sense of personal pride. I learned how to get out of my own way and let the numbers work.

So there you have it; my father furnished me with the greatest lesson

I've ever learned in sales, and he'd never been in sales. But he did know a thing or two about getting out of his own way. His father died when he was ten. His beloved mother suffered a nervous breakdown under the financial stress of trying to raise him and his siblings. Buzz didn't earn his high school diploma; he had to work two jobs to help support his family. He went off to Europe to serve his country during World War II. Upon his return, he learned some technical skills at trade school and eventually became an aerospace engineer, part of the team of people that put a man on the moon. With all of those odds stacked against him, my father was able to get out of his own way.

I lost my father in 1987. He saw some of my early success, and I know he's seen the rest of it from where he sits right now. Buzz was an inspiration to me and still is. I've been blessed to have a lot of people play a hand in my career along the way. I always tell people, "I was lucky; lucky I wasn't lazy and lucky I could follow direction."

I love the game of sales. I hope that you fall in love with it, also. It has given me just about everything I have ever dreamed of financially and otherwise, if not even a little more. This is the part of the book where I sign off and wish you luck. I hope you're lucky enough to not be lazy and lucky enough to be open to good direction. I'm not sure any sales expert or trainer will have all the answers for you. I do know that The CAP Equation©, if practiced in its pristine format, will get you where you want to go. Hey, like the man convinced me all those years ago at that chilidog stand, "It's foolproof."

Acknowledgments

This book was a labor of love. I enjoyed the writing process immensely; spending almost a year trying to get the content in my head expressed in just the right way on paper. It wasn't easy. Nobody said it would be, but it was comforting to know I had a great deal of support, and I needed that support often during the yearlong creative journey.

I reached out to a select group of old friends, a few who possessed volumes of expertise in frontline sales, sales leadership and marketing. I asked them to take a look at early versions of the manuscript. They were all gracious with their time and so clear in their opinions.

My sincere thanks to Kate Castro, she was totally on point with her recommendations and notes. She is a friend, but felt comfortable enough with me to be unfiltered in her suggestions for improvement. I asked Warren Steele to take a look at an early manuscript draft. I was interested in leveraging his Ivy League eye and C-Suite intuition. His perspective was different than some of the sales folk. His diverse viewpoint and sage advice were treasured.

My good friend, Marshall McDonald, dug through an early manuscript. Marshall's voice was an important one for me because he has one of the most pragmatic heads of anyone I've had the pleasure to work with. His views were also very important to me because, like me, he puts people first. His notes and thoughts were lucid and helped me shape a few chapters differently.

Renee Corso is not only one of the most talented salespeople I've ever known, she's also one of the most dedicated. Her thoughts were instrumental in helping me soften some hard edges that existed in the original manuscript.

Sometimes a person possesses intuition beyond their years. Jody Willis is such a person and was my 'go-to' organizational sales trainer for years, beginning the job at a tender young age. He has a talent and passion for on-boarding new sales people and his notes were the most analytical of the bunch.

I want to sincerely thank some other dear friends that weren't involved in the review of the early drafts, but were instrumental in helping me refine some of the later content that made its way into print. I want to offer a sincere thanks to Dawn Christensen for allowing me to keep her on the phone longer than she probably wanted to, and to John Birsner for his philosophical counsel on what makes a modern day salesperson tick. Tim Martin was incredibly helpful during the stretch run of this project. Tim helped me refine and expand on vital topics and content. He's someone I respect greatly; in fact, he's one of the purest sales trainers in the country. For he and I to have spent over a hundred hours this year discussing what keeps sales people and leaders up at night was incredibly valuable to me. Tim was not only instrumental from a content perspective; he also encouraged me when he sensed my confidence level was sagging. Tim is a fine writer and he knows how tough it is to create something out of nothing.

In addition to the amazing collection of friends that were there for me during the writing process, there was also a tribe of people that provided another critical element to the mix. These treasured friends were the early adopters of The CAP Equation© training methods and brand. These were the people that invited me to coach and train their valued sales teams even though my book wasn't published yet.

Brent Goode, Joe, Alan and the lovely Joanna Matherly hosted me in Nashville and I fell in love with that awesome city and their talented management team. Miriam Hungerford and Hank Yuloff both asked me to address their business organizations in 2014 and have been so gracious in their promotion of The CAP Equation©. My old friends and colleagues from the Midwest, Gary Ware and Doug Fox also served as listening ears and were valuable partners during year one.

My summer speaking tour took me to the City by the Bay where Rich Kunz had just accepted an executive sales leadership position. It was an honor to be selected as a keynote speaker at one of his first general sales meetings. Rich has been generous with his praise and also with his time. He has been a guest on more than one CAP Coaching© session. He big-heartedly offered his expertise to new and developing salespeople.

Andy Grethel is the guy you want on your team if you're a coach. You'd also want to *be* on *his* team if you were a player. He's one of the most genuine people I know and you can feel the respect people have for him. He's been lavish in his praise of our programs and a promoter of the brand. I can't thank Andy enough for his support.

Sincere thanks are in order for Dan Bredeson and his wife, Dominique. They couldn't have been more supportive of our training methodology. Dan invited me into his sales organization on several occasions. He also added fuel to my fire, keeping me accountable by sending off a text to me each week. The texts always read, "Finish the damn book!" Dan was once a protégé of mine, now he's a mentor to me.

My thanks and gratitude also goes out to Mr. Les Heinsen. Les and his wife Sharon have always been so kind and supportive to my wife and I. Our travels took us up to Reno, Nevada this summer to address his awesome team. It was during our dinner together after the event that I reflected on a specific memory. It was the recollection that I wanted to model myself after Les when I first became a sales leader with Aflac in the early 90s. The truth is that I'm still trying to model myself after him in many ways.

I want to thank Steve and Bill Harrison and their impressive team of coaches at Bradley Communications, including, Martha Bullen, Geoffrey Berwind, Brian Edmondson and Raia King. There are many facets of creating and marketing a book and that tremendous team was only a phone call away whenever we got stuck. Through our association with Bradley Communications my wife and I were able to spend a few days with the great Jack Canfield. Of course, Jack is the co-creator of the *Chicken Soup for the Soul* book series and the best selling author of *The Success Principles*. To have one of the best selling non-fiction authors of all time review your work and offer advice was priceless.

The most convincing thing Jack said to me during our time together was, "It occurs to me that you are looking for an invitation to a party that you're already at." This was Jack's way of telling me I belonged being a successful author, speaker and sales trainer. His slightly sardonic comment didn't fall on deaf ears and it reminded me that I might have to get out of my own way. Thanks for that little nugget, Jack.

A very talented lady, Madalyn Stone, stepped into the breach and delivered a nicely polished manuscript when all was said and done. She was effusive in her praise of what didn't need fixing and equally straightforward in her quest to point out what needed my attention. Her notes were extremely well thought out and there were few, if any, of her suggestions that I didn't take action on. I would also like to thank Jerry and Michele Dorris at AuthorSupport.com for their fine design work. Their expertise puts a nice bow on this package.

If I don't count my two male, yellow Labradors, Buzz and Ozzy, I am the sole dude living in my home. But, there are two lovely female distractions living there too. My daughter, Alyssa, is sixteen years old going on twenty-nine. She has a quick wit and a sharp tongue, as a lot of her kind does. She is a concert Violist, (having already performed at Carnegie Hall), and she's an All League high school golfer. She carries a 4.0 GPA and is a darn good photographer, video editor, web designer, graphic designer, music industry blogger and Mac genius. I'm fairly sure she could fly the Space Shuttle if they let her, but for now I just let her borrow my car so she can drive herself to school.

I want to thank Alyssa for offering encouraging words to me (albeit under her breath), and for knowing that when I'm sitting, staring at the screen of my laptop, eyes glazed over, it's probably not the right time to ask me to hang yet another My Chemical Romance poster on her wall. I love you, Bear!

Behind every great man, there should be a great woman, or vice versa. But I know that, in the real world, it isn't always that way. Regardless of your relationship status, if you're lucky enough to have a supportive partner, well...you are much more than *lucky*. I have an incredible wife. I don't take her for granted anymore. I think I used to. I was running a hundred miles an hour earlier in our marriage, trying to stay close to the top rung of the corporate ladder. I'm not anymore. I'm around the house more often now.

I want to thank Beth Buzzello for so many things. If I listed them all, this acknowledgement section would go way over the standard page count. I will refrain from the entire list and focus on the few things that were most impactful in the creation of my first non-fiction publication.

Thank you, Beth, for telling me that the book was going to be great and that I'm a good writer. That was needed when those terrible, but inevitable, writers' doubts crept into my brain. Thanks for reminding me how important this work is, saying things like, "Hey, people are telling you that your work is changing their careers...get back to work." Thanks for doing an exhaustive initial edit on this book, and for being honest enough to tell me some things didn't fit, didn't belong in the manuscript.

I would be remiss if I didn't thank Beth for holding everything together as I endeavored to reinvent myself as an author, speaker and trainer. Lastly, I want to thank her for waking up each morning with a smile on her face, and for reminding me that life is good. She is by far, the nicest, sweetest, kindest, most well adjusted person I know. Nobody else even comes close.

Okay, all of the acknowledgments are done.

Let's go sell something!

LINKS • RESOURCES • COACHING • SPEAKING

FOLLOW JOE BUZZELLO AT:

Facebook–https://www.facebook.com/Joebuzz
Twitter–https://twitter.com/JoeBuzzello
LinkedIn–http://www.linkedin.com/in/JoeBuzzello

FOLLOW THE CAP EQUATION© AT:

Home Site–http://www.thecapequation.com/access/
Facebook–https://www.facebook.com/TheCAPequation
Twitter–https://twitter.com/capequation

RESOURCES *(That Support This Book)*

Throughout this book we've suggested that you visit The CAP Equation© website to obtain various resources that will help you gain the most from these teachings. If you haven't grabbed these valuable resources yet, now's the time! You simply enter your first name and email address. There is no cost.

Go here: http://www.thecapequation.com/resources/

If you have a QR code reader on your mobile device, then please go here:

Free Resources

To Support This Book

CAP COACHING© *(Live-Group, Frontline and Leadership)*

The CAP Equation© community offers you access to free and premium LIVE tele-seminar coaching programs. For complete information on program details and schedules please go to:

http://www.thecapequation.com/coaching/

THE CAP EQUATION© KEYNOTE SPEAKING AND WORKSHOPS

Joe Buzzello has delivered his powerful message to outside sales professionals and network marketers around the country. For a complete menu of speaking and workshop topics and to contact Joe, please go to:

http://www.thecapequation.com/speaking/